EASY MAGIC

Karl Fulves

Illustrated by

Joseph K. Schmidt

DOVER PUBLICATIONS, INC.
New York

Bibliographical Note

Easy Magic is a new work, first published by Dover Publications, Inc., in 1995.

Library of Congress Cataloging-in-Publication Data

Fulves, Karl.
    Easy magic / Karl Fulves ; illustrated by Joseph K. Schmidt
        p.   cm.
    ISBN 0-486-28622-3
    1. Conjuring.   2. Tricks.   I. Title.
GV1555.F85   1995
793.8—dc20   95-118
                                                                            CIP

Manufactured in the United States of America
Dover Publications, Inc., 31 East 2nd Street, Mineola, N.Y. 11501

Introduction

For a long time magic was difficult to master. Secrets were well kept and expensive, tricks depended on complicated sleight of hand to work and few tricks appeared in book form.

All that has changed. Magic tricks have been streamlined. Many are easy to perform. New books on the subject describe magic secrets in clear detail. This book is a collection of modern magic tricks that are easy to do, but mystifying and entertaining as well.

Although these tricks are simple, there are a few guidelines that add to their impact.

Practice tricks so you can perform them without having to stop and think what comes next. When the working is automatic, you know you are ready to perform the trick before an audience.

The magician's term *"Patter"* refers to the words you use when performing a trick. Choose patter that ties in with current events, popular cartoon characters or recent movies. Libraries stock book collections of gags and jokes. Pick out a few jokes to enliven your patter. Comedians and speech writers consult such books all the time because they are a valuable source of material.

Many books on magic instruct the reader to *practice before a mirror* because the mirror shows the trick as the audience sees it. When you perform a trick before the mirror, look for ways to make your handling of apparatus as clear as possible. For example, a trick may say that you start by displaying a coin in your left hand. As you can see in Figure *A*, the coin is clearly visible from your point of view. But when you view it in the mirror, you see that the fingers hide the coin. This tells you that the audience cannot see clearly what you hold in your hand.

If the left hand is positioned so that the fingers point more toward the floor, the audience gets a clear view of the coin, Figure *B*. The opposite situation holds when you want to conceal an object in the hand. When you view the situation in front of the

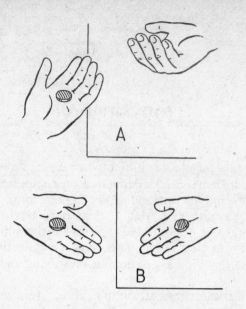

A

B

mirror, check to make sure that, if the hand is held in a certain way, the object is concealed from audience view. Remember to hold the hand that way when doing the trick.

As a magician, your performance should be governed by two rules. First, do not tell how a trick is done. Magic tricks are designed with only one goal: to entertain audiences with the performance of seemingly inexplicable feats. If a magic secret is revealed, it defeats the very purpose for which it was intended. Your reputation as a magician is enhanced if you keep the secret.

Second, do not repeat tricks. A few tricks are designed to be repeated; they gain in strength when done over again. But most tricks have been invented for a one-time-only performance. When someone says, "Do that again," he is telling you he was fooled. To keep him fooled, move on to another trick.

Many of the tricks in this book can be done at parties. Some can be performed for larger audiences. For example, if your school or local club has a talent contest, pick a trick like "The Vanishing Ring" (No. 37), which can be seen by a large audience. You may not win every contest, but you can be sure your act will be remembered.

KARL FULVES

Contents

Tricks with Cards

No area of legerdemain is more popular than card magic. Each year hundreds of new card tricks are developed. Some of the best are easy to do and can be learned by anyone willing to take the time to master the details of the handling. Newcomers to magic frequently start out by performing simple card tricks for friends. Fortunately, there is now a wide selection of baffling card mysteries that can be performed under almost any circumstances.

Most of the card tricks in this chapter can be performed with any borrowed deck of cards. A few require slight preparation, but that small amount of preparation sets up big mysteries. Remember to practice so that you can perform each trick smoothly.

1. No Guesswork

In this puzzling mystery, you seem to make an accurate prediction even though you have no advance information to go on. Deal two heaps of cards face down on the table, Figure 1. While you

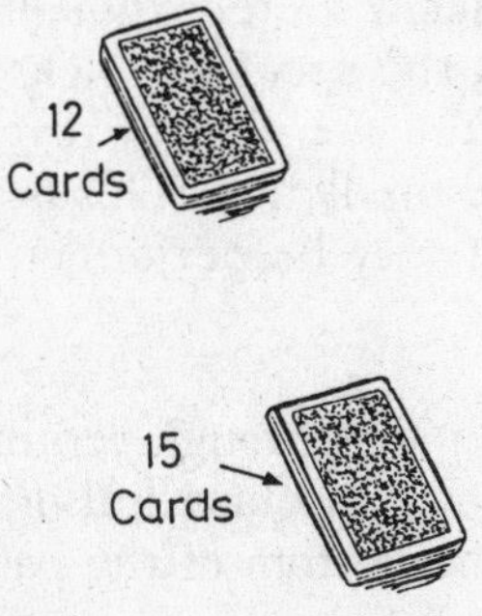

12 Cards

15 Cards

Fig. 1

turn your head aside, ask the spectator to take some cards from the heap nearest him. When he has done this, turn around and pick up the heap nearest you.

Say, "I don't know how many cards you have." Point to your heap of cards. "But I know that I have the *same* number of cards you have, *plus* enough more to make twelve, *plus* three left over."

You and he count your cards. Your prediction is correct even though you really do not know how many cards the spectator chose.

Method: Deal 12 cards in front of the spectator. Deal 15 cards to yourself. Do not count the cards out loud when you deal. You want the spectator to think you are using a random number of cards.

Turn your head aside. Ask him to take away some cards from the 12-card heap. He can take from one to 11 cards. He puts those cards to one side.

After he has done this, turn and face him. Pick up the 15-card heap. The words you say are the same each time, no matter how many cards he has. Say, "I don't know how many cards you have, but I know that I have the same number you have, plus enough more to make twelve, plus three left over."

Ask the spectator to count his cards into a heap. Say he has ten cards. Count ten cards from the top of your packet to satisfy your claim that you have as many as he does. Count enough more to make 12 (thus satisfying your second claim). Finally, count the remaining three cards to satisfy your third claim.

2. Secret Thought

The revelation of a card merely thought of is an entertaining novelty. In this trick the spectator picks a card so that only he knows its identity. You are able to reveal the chosen card by means of an infallible prediction. This is a good trick to perform at a party because it may be performed at any time with borrowed cards.

Method: Remove the ace through ten of clubs from the deck. Arrange them face down in numerical order with the ace at the top and the ten at the bottom of the packet. Then remove the

♦ 10 and place it under the card box. Don't let anyone see the face of this card.

Turn your back. Ask the spectator to lift off a bunch of cards from the top of the deck. It can be any number from one to ten. Have him count the cards and remember the number. Say he removed seven cards. Ask him to hide this packet in his pocket.

Turn and face him. Spread the club packet on the table so he can see the faces of all ten cards. Say, "Whatever number of cards you have, remember the club with that number. In other words, if you have two cards, you would remember the two of clubs, if you have eight cards in your pocket, you would remember the eight of clubs. Don't tell anyone the name of your card."

In our example the spectator would think of the ♣7. Pick up the club packet and remove the ace. Glance at it as if looking for clues. Then place it face down on top of the deck. Do the same with the 2, then the 3, then the 4, and so on, placing each card on top of the deck. It appears as if you are studying the cards, but you are actually reversing their order. When you have completed this process, the ♣10 will be the top card of the deck.

The patter line is, "Think of your card. I want to see if I can pick it up by means of thought waves. Let's see, I believe you are thinking of a black card." Say this with a smile as a joke; after all, *all* the cards are black cards, so you cannot be wrong. Then say, "I'm going out on a limb and say you picked a club." Again there is no surprise; all ten cards are clubs.

Say, "Please remove the cards from your pocket and replace them on top of the deck." When the spectator has done this, say, "I put a card under the card box. This is the card that will help me find your card."

Turn the card face up to show the ♦10. "This ten-spot tells me to deal ten cards off the top of the deck." Deal ten cards into a heap on the table. "What card did you pick?"

The spectator says he picked the ♣7. Turn over the top card of the deck to reveal the ♣7.

3. Think of a Card

This is an easy-to-do card trick that allows you to reveal any card thought of by the spectator.

Beforehand, secretly place any two, three and five-spot in to your pocket. That is the only preparation. When ready to perform the trick, ask the spectator to shuffle the deck. Then have him spread the cards so he can see the faces. He removes any card from the deck and holds it so he alone can see the face of the card.

Take back the rest of the deck and put it in your pocket. Reach into your pocket and pretend to remove a random card. In reality, take the two-spot. Show it and say, "Whatever the value of your card, multiply it by the value of this card." He can do this in his head or with the aid of pencil and paper. (Jacks count as 11, queens as 12 and kings as 13.)

Pretend to remove another random card. Really take the three-spot out of your pocket. Show the card to the spectator. Say, "Add the value of this card to your number."

When he has done this, remove the five-spot. "Whatever the value of this card, multiply it by your number."

Finally, ask the spectator to add 1 if his card is a club, 2 if it is a diamond, 3 if it is a heart and 4 if it is a spade. When he has the sum, he tells it to you. You then go on to reveal the chosen card.

To determine the spectator's card, subtract 15 from the total he gives you. You will have a two-digit or a three-digit result. The first one or two digits tells you the value of his card. The final digit tells you the suit.

Let us assume he picked the ♠K. The arithmetic would look like this:

$$
\begin{aligned}
\text{Multiply the value by 2:} \quad 13 \times 2 &= 26. \\
\text{Add 3:} \quad 26 + 3 &= 29. \\
\text{Multiply the sum by 5:} \quad 29 \times 5 &= 145. \\
\text{Add the value of the suit:} \quad 145 + 4 &= 149.
\end{aligned}
$$

When this total is announced to you, subtract 15, getting

$$149 - 15 = 134.$$

The first two digits tell you he picked a card with a value of 13, or a king. The final digit, a 4, tells you he picked a spade. Announce that the chosen card is the ♠K. The fact that you do not seem to know which cards you randomly remove from your pocket makes this a seemingly genuine test in mind reading.

4. The Lie Detector

"This deck of cards has been programmed so it can tell when someone is lying or telling the truth." As you speak, have the cards shuffled, turn your back and let someone choose a card at random. The spectator can lie or tell the truth in answer to a question you ask him, but the cards sort out truth from falsehood and produce the chosen card every time.

Method: Ask someone to shuffle the deck. Turn your back. Have the spectator deal nine cards onto the table. He shuffles the cards and turns the packet face up. Ask him to remember the face card of the packet. In Figure 2 that would be the ♦ 2.

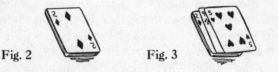

Fig. 2   Fig. 3

Keeping your back turned, ask him to deal two cards face up from the deck onto his card, Figure 3. Finally, have him turn the entire packet face down.

Turn and face the spectator. Take the packet from him. Say, "I'm going to ask you for the color of your card. You can tell the truth or you can lie. For example, if your card is red, you can tell the truth and say it is a red card or you can lie and say it is a black card. What was the color of your card?"

It does not matter how he responds. Whatever the spectator's reply, you spell that color by dealing a card at a time for each letter from the top to the bottom of the packet. Then state the color and deal the next card to the table. Do this until you are left with one card. It will be the spectator's card.

For example, if the spectator said his card was red, spell R-E-D, dealing a card for each letter from the top to the bottom of the packet. Then say, "red," and deal the top card of the packet to the table. Spell R-E-D again, dealing a card from the top to the bottom of the packet for each letter. Again say, "red," and deal the top card to the table. Continue until one card is left in your hand. Whether the spectator lied or told the truth about the color of his card, the card remaining in your hand will always be the chosen card.

5. Sum and Difference

In this remarkable card effect you appear to know the sum and difference of two random cards chosen from a shuffled pack.

Method: Before the performance, secretly place any king in your jacket or trouser pocket. That is the only preparation.

When ready to present "Sum and Difference," hand the deck to the spectator. Invite him to shuffle it until he is confident the deck is well mixed. Ask him to cut a packet of cards off the top of the deck. The packet should contain at least 12 or 13 cards.

Take the packet and place it in your pocket as you say, "I want to isolate the cards for a moment so I can concentrate." The pocket you place the cards in is the pocket that has the king in it.

Pretend to think deep thoughts, then write the number 26 on a piece of paper without showing it to anyone. Fold the paper in half and in half again. Drop it into a glass so it is in full view.

Remove the packet from your pocket. Make sure you take the king out with the packet. Give the cards a quick shuffle so the king is lost in the packet.

Hand the packet to the spectator. Say, "I'd like you to remove the card that has the highest value and the card that has the lowest value. Aces count low and kings count high. Jacks have a value of eleven, queens a value of twelve, and kings a value of thirteen. If there are two or more cards of the same value, pick the one that seems to stand out."

When the spectator has removed the two cards, say, "I'd like you to add the highest-value card to the lowest-value card and write down the sum. Then subtract the lowest-value card from the highest-value card and write down the difference. Add the sum to the difference. What total do you get?"

He will always arrive at a total of 26. Have him open the paper and verify that your prediction is correct.

To take one example, suppose he picks a king and a seven. He adds them together to get $13 + 7 = 20$. Then he subtracts them, getting $13 - 7 = 6$. When he adds $20 + 6$, he arrives at 26.

The predicted number is always twice as much as the largest value card. You can perform the trick at a moment's notice without preparation if you are willing to take a chance. Write "26" as your prediction. Ask the spectator to shuffle the deck and cut it in thirds. Ask him to take the highest-value card from one pile and the lowest-value card from another. You are taking a chance here that there is a king in each heap. If the first heap he picks contains a king, the outcome will agree with your prediction. If not, say that you would like to try another prediction. Pick a trick like "Secret Thought" (No. 2) and you will always succeed.

6. I've Got Your Number

This is a triple mystery that packs a punch. A group of face-up cards is shuffled into a group of face-down cards by a spectator. He mixes the cards until he is satisfied they are well shuffled.

While you turn your back, he divides the cards into two equal heaps. He gives you either heap behind your back. Turn and face him. "I wanted to get an impression of the cards you gave me, but I decided to do it the hard way, without looking at the cards." Pause as if to receive psychic vibrations. "I think I've got it. If I add the number of face-up cards in my packet to the number of face-down cards in your packet, the total is exactly nine."

Bring your cards into view. You may have four face-up cards. The spectator has five face-down cards. The total of 4 and 5 is 9, matching your prediction exactly.

When you repeat the trick, you claim that your face-up cards added to his face-down cards will total 10. When the cards are counted, you are again correct.

Finally you do something much harder. This time you predict that you will have the *same* number of face-up cards he has and the *same* number of face-down cards. The cards are counted and once again you are correct.

Method: Put 3 face-up cards into your jacket sleeve or into a back pocket ahead of time. The audience is unaware of this secret preparation.

When you perform the trick, remove 16 cards from the deck. Turn eight of them face up. Ask the spectator to shuffle the two groups together. He can shuffle the cards several times. Make sure he does not accidentally turn any cards over.

Turn your back. Ask him to deal the cards into two packets of eight cards each. He gives you either packet behind your back. After a moment of thought, state that your face-up cards, added to his face-down cards, will total exactly 9. As you speak, secretly turn over your packet. Slide one of the face-up cards out of your sleeve and add it to the top of the packet. Bring your cards into view. Deal the cards off the top one at a time. Deal the face-up cards to the table. Deal the face-down cards to the top of the deck to get them out of the way.

Ask the spectator to count his face-down cards and add them to your face-up cards. He will get a total of 9, just as you predicted.

You are going to repeat the trick, but with a difference. Turn all of the cards face-down and return them to the top of the deck. Deal off 16 cards. Turn eight of them face up and have the spectator shuffle this group into the face-down group. While you turn your back, the spectator divides the cards into two heaps of eight cards each. He gives you either heap behind your back.

Facing him, say, "This time, if we add my face-up cards to your face-down cards, the total will be exactly 10." As you speak, secretly turn your packet over. Then add two face-up cards from your sleeve or back pocket to the top of the packet.

Bring your cards into view. As before, deal the face-up cards to the table. Deal the face-down cards to the top of the deck so they are out of the way. Have the spectator count the face-down cards he has and add them to the face-up cards from your packet. The total will be 10, as you predicted.

For the final trick, turn all cards face down and replace them on top of the deck. Deal 16 cards off the top. Turn eight of them face up. Ask the spectator to mix them with the face-down cards.

Turn your back. Have the spectator divide the cards into two equal heaps as before. He gives you either heap behind your back. Turn to him and say, "This time, I have the *same* number of face-up cards you have, and further, I have the *same* number of face-down cards as you have." Turn your packet over.

Bring your cards into view. The spectator counts your face-up cards. He has the same number of face-up cards. He counts your face-down cards, and discovers he has the same number of face-down cards!

7. Stock-Market Magic

"Here is a chance to play the stock market and make a profit. I'm going to see if I can act the part of a market prognosticator and predict the outcome." You ask three people to "play the stock market" with cards while you turn your back. You succeed in correctly predicting how many cards they started with (a number you could not possibly know in advance) and you tell one player exactly how much profit he made playing the market. This trick is impromptu and uses any deck of cards.

Method: When the cards are handed to you, remove the top six cards from the deck and place them inside the card box. Do not call attention to the number of cards.

Turn your back. State that you would like three spectators to play the stock market. "You should all start with an equal number of stocks. Silently deal the same number of cards to each person playing the market. It can be any number. To make it more interesting, make sure it's more than five cards each."

Let's say the three players are Ben, Kim and Frank. You do not know how many cards each player gets, but we will assume for this example, that each gets ten cards.

"Kim lost three shares on Monday. Kim, place three cards in the card box." When Kim has done this, she will have seven cards left.

"On Tuesday Frank lost two shares. Frank, put two cards in the card box." After Frank has done this, he will have eight cards.

"Ben did well on Wednesday. Remove four cards from the card box and give them to Ben." When this has been done, Ben will have 14 cards.

"Ben saw that Frank needed financial help. Frank, silently count the number of cards you have. Whisper the number to Ben. I'd like Ben to give Frank a number of cards equal to the number that Frank already has." In our example, Frank has eight cards, so Ben would give Frank eight more cards. Frank now has 16 cards.

"I didn't forget about Kim. When we started, I made a prediction by putting some cards inside the card box. Kim, I'd like you and Frank to combine your cards. Then empty the cards out of the card box and add them to your pile."

When this has been done, say, "Good. Now deal out three equal heaps of cards." After this has been done, say, "How many cards did each of you start with? Ten? Count the number of cards in each heap and you will find that you each have exactly ten cards again."

When this has been verified, say, "Ben, you are the only one with some extra cards, so let's see if I can guess what kind of profit you made on the stock market. I'd guess you have made a profit of six cards, right? Thank you!"

Just remember to place six cards inside the card box at the start. No matter how many cards each player started with, Ben will always have six extra cards at the finish.

8. What's in a Name?

Removing a packet of cards from the deck, you say to a spectator, "Give me your best friend's first name." Let's say he replies, "Neal." Say, "That name is a real standout. Here's what I mean."

The spectator spells N-E-A-L, dealing a card from the top to the bottom of the packet for each letter. He then turns the top card face up on top of the packet. He repeats this process of dealing and spelling the name, then turning up the top card, until only one face-down card is left.

"You could have picked any name, but you picked a name that stands by itself. All of the cards you turned face up are black. Look at the one remaining face-down card."

When the spectator turns that card over it is a red-backed ace, the *only* red card in the packet.

Method: Holding the deck so only you can see the faces, remove ten black cards and place them in a face-down heap on the table. Then remove a red ace and place it on top of the heap. Hand this 11-card packet to the spectator.

Ask him to pick a name. He can pick a name that is spelled with two to ten letters. This covers most of the names he is likely to choose, but if he picks a longer name, such as Bartholomew, tell him that you will both grow old by the time he finishes spelling this name ten times; ask him to pick a name that is spelled with fewer letters.

When he has decided on a name, he spells the name, transferring a card from top to bottom for each letter. After he has finished spelling the name, ask him to turn the top card face up and replace it on top of the packet.

He spells the name again, transferring a card at a time from top to bottom for each letter. When he has finished, have him turn the top card face up and replace it on top.

He repeats this process until there is only one face-down card left. It will always be the red ace.

9. The Computer Deck

You can turn your deck of cards into a temporary computer with this surprising trick. The spectator cuts the deck into four packets. You run through a computer program and produce the four aces.

Method: Place the four aces on top of the deck. Then transfer the bottom card of the deck to the top. The aces are thus second, third, fourth and fifth from the top of the deck. This preparation is done secretly. If you wish to perform other tricks first, you can leave this five-card stack inside the card box. Do a few tricks with the rest of the deck. Tricks like "No Guesswork" (No. 1) and "What's in a Name" (No. 8) described earlier in this chapter, are ideal. When you are ready to perform "The Computer Deck," put the cards in the card box so that the five-card stack is loaded onto the top of the deck. Then pretend to remember one more trick. Remove the deck and perform "The Computer Deck."

Explain to the spectator that you have discovered computer software that turns a deck of cards into a computer.

Ask the spectator to cut the deck into two approximately equal heaps. When he does this, keep track of the top half, that is, the portion containing the aces. Then ask the spectator to cut each of the packets in half. You now have four packets of cards. Arrange the four packets in a row so that the heap containing the aces is on the right, Figure 4.

Fig. 4

"This is how the program works." Pick up the packet on the left. "This is packet number one, so we transfer one card from top to bottom." As you say this, take the top card of the packet and place it on the bottom of the packet.

"Then we deal one to each of the other packets." Deal the top card to the top of packet No. 2, the next card to the top of packet No. 3, and the next card to the top of packet No. 4. Replace packet No. 1 back in its original position.

Pick up the next packet and say, "This is packet number two, so we transfer two cards." Deal two cards from the top to the bottom of this packet. Then deal a card to the top of each of the other packets. Replace this packet on the table.

Pick up the next packet and say, "This is packet number three, so we transfer three cards." Deal three cards from the top to the bottom of this packet. Then deal a card to the top of each of the other packets. Replace this packet on the table.

"And this is packet number four, so we transfer four cards." Now you pick up the last heap, the one with the aces in it. Transfer the top four cards to the bottom of the packet. Deal a card off the top to each of the other three heaps. Replace this packet on the table.

"That's how the program works. It's great for games like poker." Turn up the top card of each heap to reveal that the program produced the four aces.

It Figures

The belief that numbers influence a person's life is the study of numerology. The tricks in this chapter use a variety of objects, but they are all concerned with numbers. Pocket calculators make it easy to perform the simple calculations called for in these tricks. By including a number trick in your magic performance, you add an intriguing element of novelty.

10. Think of a Number

Ask a spectator to think of any number and enter it into a pocket calculator. Ask him to multiply the number by 2, add 12, divide by 2, subtract the original number and remember the answer. For example:

Think of any number 5
Multiply it by 2 .... $5 \times 2 = 10$
Add 12 .... $10 + 12 = 22$
Divide by 2 .... $22 \div 2 = 11$
Subtract the original number .... $11 - 5 = 6$
Remember the answer 6

Fig. 5

No matter what number the spectator has chosen, the answer will always be 6. Pretend you do not know the answer.

Jot down the digits from 1 to 10 on a piece of paper as shown in Figure 5. Hand the pad to the spectator. Ask him to look over the numbers, find his number and imagine that a circle has been drawn around that number. Turn your head aside while he does this.

Take back the pad. Pretend to concentrate on the numbers. Then pick up a pencil and draw a circle around the number 6. Say, "In your thoughts you pictured a circle around your number. Did it look like this?" Turn the pad around and show him that you circled the correct number.

If you are asked to repeat the trick, in the step where you ask the spectator to add a number, instead of having him add 12, have him add 14. The result will be the digit 7, which you will circle on the paper. Since this is a different number from the one he got the first time, he will have no clue as to how you knew his number.

11. Iced Dice

Dice are available in many board games. They can also be obtained in stationery stores. For this puzzling trick you will need three dice and a paper bag.

While you turn your back, the spectator rolls two dice and stacks one on top of the other. He then covers the stacked dice with a paper bag.

Turn and face the spectator. Picking up the third die, you roll it a few times, then place it under the bag and on top of the stack.

You then jot down a number on a piece of paper, fold the paper and place it in plain view. Ask the spectator to lift the bag. He is to add together the numbers on the top and bottom of each die, and then he is to subtract the topmost number on the top die, since it is the most visible number.

The spectator might arrive at a total of 19. He reads your prediction. You correctly foretold that the total would be 19. The trick may be repeated. The total is different each time, yet you are always correct.

Method: You do not need to know the numbers on the spectator's dice. When you place the third die under the bag and on top of the stack, note the top number on this die. Subtract this number from 21 and write the result as your prediction. In Figure 6, your die is placed on the stack with the number 2 uppermost. Subtract 2 from 21 to arrive at 19.

Fig. 6

When the spectator adds together the top and bottom numbers on all three dice, and then subtracts the top number on the top die, he will arrive at a total of 19.

If you are asked to repeat the trick, place the third die on top of the stack with a different number showing on top. Subtract this number from 21 to arrive at your new total.

12. Figure Fun

You can reveal a secretly chosen number under seemingly impossible conditions. The spectator arrives at a number by a random process. He jots down the number on a piece of paper and covers it with a cup or mug, Figure 7. Turning around and glancing at the cup, you reveal the hidden number.

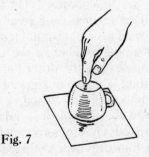

Fig. 7

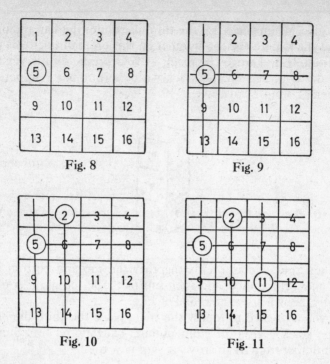

Fig. 8

Fig. 9

Fig. 10

Fig. 11

Method: On a piece of paper draw a 4 × 4 layout of squares and number the squares from 1 to 16, Figure 8. Hand the spectator a pencil and turn your back.

Ask him to circle a number in the first column. In the example we will use here, he circles the number 5 as indicated in Figure 8.

Ask him to draw a line through the other numbers in that same vertical column, and the other numbers in that same horizontal row. This is shown in Figure 9.

Ask him to draw a circle around one of the remaining numbers in the second column. Say he chooses 2. He then draws a line through the other numbers in that same column, and the other numbers in that same row. This is shown in Figure 10.

Now he circles a remaining number in the third column. Say he picks 11. He then crosses out the other numbers in that column and row. The situation is shown in Figure 11.

There will be one number left uncrossed in the final column. He circles that number. In our example it is the number 16.

Ask him to add up the four chosen numbers. He will get 5 + 2 + 11 + 16 = 34. Have him turn over the paper, write the total, and cover it with a cup. Turn and face the spectator. Glance at

16

the cup, pretend you have x-ray vision, then announce that the total is 34. You will be correct because the total is always 34, no matter which numbers he picks.

13. Number Magic

In this subtle mystery you are able to reveal two numbers chosen by the spectator. The spectator shuffles the deck and hands it to you behind your back. He cuts off a group of cards, then another group. He takes the top card and remembers its value.

With your back still turned, you ask him to enter that number into a pocket calculator. Then ask him to think of another number and multiply it by the first.

When he has done this, you take the calculator. The display might show the number 296. Doing some psychic figuring, you reveal that the first number he chose was 8 and the second number 37.

Method: After the spectator has shuffled the deck, glimpse the bottom card. Say it is an eight-spot. It is not necessary to remember the suit. Hold the deck behind your back. Ask the spectator to cut off about a third of the deck.

When he has done this, turn and face him. Say, "That's not quite enough. Take a few more." While you are facing him, the deck is out of sight behind your back. Silently transfer the bottom card (the eight-spot in our example) to the top of the deck. Then turn your back to the spectator.

He cuts off a few more cards and places them on top of the cards he has already. Ask him to look at the top card and enter that number in the calculator. This number must be the value of the card you glimpsed, in this case 8. Ask him to think of another number and multiply it by the first number. After he has done this, take back the calculator.

Divide the number in the display by 8 (or whatever card you glimpsed on the bottom of the deck). The number now showing in the calculator display is the second number. Since you already know the first number, you can reveal each in dramatic fashion. For example, you can say, "This morning I saw a sports car driving down the street. The license-plate number was eight dash thirty-seven. It struck me at the time that those numbers would be important. Did you pick eight and thirty-seven by any chance?"

14. Murder by Calculation

Entering a home in which a murder had been committed, the police were baffled. In the victim's wallet were pictures of the victim's closest friends and most likely suspects—Lil Bell, Bo Ellis, Bob Hill and Bill Lee. Scrawled on a piece of paper was a mysterious number. Working from these clues, and using nothing more than a pocket calculator, you, playing the part of the detective, solve the mystery.

Method: To prepare for this entertaining mystery, make up four cards like those shown in Figure 12. The name Lil Bell is printed on one side; the number 773-8717 is written on the back. Proceed in the same way with the other names and numbers. Besides these cards, you will need a pocket calculator that has an eight-digit display.

| LIL BELL | BO ELLIS | BOB HILL | BILL LEE |

773-8717   517-7308   771-4808   337-7718

Fig. 12

Tell the story described above. As you do, mix the cards and deal them to the table so the number side of each card is uppermost. Ask the spectator to choose one. Place this card under a book. As you do, say, "The murderer went into hiding." If you have a murder-mystery book handy, place the chosen card under that to add a bit of atmosphere to the trick.

Say, "In the victim's wallet were these names and phone numbers." As you speak, turn each of the other three cards over. Let's say they bear the names Bo Ellis, Bob Hill and Bill Lee.

"Scrawled on a piece of paper near the victim's body was a number." Write the number 2-400-8551 on a piece of paper. "Obviously it was part of a long-distance telephone number. We later traced it to the Numerology Club, where the victim met with friends. I knew immediately it was a calculated act of murder." As you say "calculated," bring out the pocket calculator.

"I had to do some fast figuring if I wanted to nab the culprit." Enter the number from the paper into the calculator: 24008551.

Point to the first of the three cards the spectator did not choose. In our example that would be Bo Ellis. Say, "I know Bo Ellis didn't do it. He was at the Numero Uno Restaurant that night." Turn the Bo Ellis card over. Subtract the number on the back from the number in the calculator. In our example you would get:

$$24008551 - 5177308 = 18831243.$$

Turn over the next card. "Bob Hill was seen at the Long Division Invitational, so he had an ironclad alibi." Turn over the Bob Hill card. Subtract the number on the back from the number showing in the calculator:

$$18831243 - 7714808 = 11116435.$$

Point to the last card. "Bill Lee is a fellow magician, so we *know* he's innocent." Turn over this card. Subtract the number on the back from the number showing in the calculator:

$$11116435 - 33777718 = 7738717.$$

Turn the calculator end for end. The number 7738717 changes into two words as shown in Figure 13. Reading the upside-down 8 as the letter B, the letters spell Lil Bell. Say, "No matter how you look at it, Lil Bell was the guilty party."

Point to the card chosen by the spectator at the start of the trick. When it is turned over, it contains Lil Bell's name.

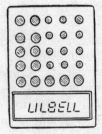

Fig. 13

Out of Sight

There are a number of strong magical effects that occur when the apparatus is out of sight momentarily. This may happen when the magician places the apparatus behind his back. It could also happen when the spectator holds the apparatus; he closes his eyes for a moment, and then opens them to discover that a magical transformation has taken place. These and other "out of sight" magical mysteries are the subject of this chapter.

15. Trisecting the Paper

A stunt impossible to solve is accomplished by magic. Tear a piece of paper almost into thirds, Figure 14. Ask the spectator to hold one of the end pieces in each hand. By pulling his hands apart, he is to cause the paper to tear into three pieces. It looks easy, but when the spectator tries it, he will find that only one piece tears off, Figure 15. The result is the same no matter how often he tries.

State that you can accomplish the feat by magic. Hold a piece of paper between the hands as shown in Figure 14. Then have the spectator grasp your wrists. Remark that you will need an interval of darkness; ask him to close his eyes. When he opens his eyes a moment later, you are holding one segment of paper in each hand, and the third segment is on the table. You have succeeded in doing the impossible.

If the spectator thinks you have somehow switched papers, even though he held your wrists, you can have him write his name across the paper so the paper cannot be switched. It makes no difference. You still succeed in tearing the paper into thirds.

Fig. 14

Fig. 15

Method: The trick is impromptu and can be performed at any time, but it must be performed for only one spectator. Anyone else present would see how the trick was done unless he also closed his eyes.

When the spectator grasps your wrists as shown in Figure 16, instruct him to close his eyes and turn his head aside so you have an interval of darkness to perform your magic.

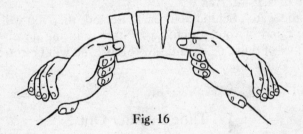

Fig. 16

When he has done this, silently lean forward and grasp the center segment of the paper between your teeth or lips. This holds it in place, allowing you to tear away the segment on the left, then the segment on the right. Let the center segment fall from your lips to the table. The trick may be repeated with a signed piece of paper.

16. Time Out

Remove your wristwatch. Ask the spectator to look at his watch and pick out an interval of time, i.e., 10, 20, 30, 40 or 50 seconds. Say he picks 30 seconds.

"It would be easy for me to tell you when thirty seconds have elapsed if I look at the second hand of my watch. It is harder to do if the watch is behind my back."

Place the watch behind your back. "Okay, look at your watch to see how close I get to thirty seconds. I'm going to start *now*."

After an interval, you say "Stop." The spectator checks his watch; you did stop 30 seconds after you started. The trick may be repeated with a different time interval.

Method: You do not get the information from your watch. You get it from your pulse. To take your pulse, place your right fingertips against your left wrist and you will feel a pulse. If you have trouble, ask a friend to show you how it is done.

Consult your watch and see how many pulse beats you feel during an interval of 10 seconds, 20 seconds and so on, up to 50 seconds. Remember these numbers.

To present the trick, check that the spectator's watch has a second hand. Remove your watch and hold it behind your back. Ask him to pick a time interval—10 seconds, 20 seconds, 30 seconds, etc. Whatever he chooses, you know how many pulse beats there are in that interval.

Take the watch behind your back. Remark that you will try to read the mind of your watch. Say, "Start counting now." Count the number of pulse beats and say, "Stop." You will be correct (or nearly so) every time.

17. Time Further Out

Ask a spectator to set his watch at any time. He hands you the watch behind your back. Say, "What time did you set it at?" Suppose the watch was set at 9:32.

"Without looking, I'm going to reset your watch so it will show a time one hour later, in other words, 10:32."

When you hand the spectator back his watch, it has indeed been set one hour later.

Method: When you are handed the watch behind your back, gently pull out the winding stem. Grasp it in one hand. Grasp the watch itself with the other hand, Figure 17. The right thumb is on top of the watch, the fingers below.

Turn the watch over, Figure 18. Since you hold the stem, the

Fig. 17   Fig. 18

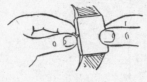

Fig. 19

watch is moving around the stem, so the watch hands must move. Grasp the watch as shown in Figure 19 so the right thumb is back on top.

Holding the stem securely with the left hand, turn the watch over again with the right hand. Once again the watch hands will move.

With many watches, when the watch has been turned around one full revolution as described above, the hands will advance one full hour. Different watches have different internal mechanisms, so you may be a bit off the first time you try it, but you can make the adjustment when you try again. Note also whether the hands move forward or back when the watch is revolved in the direction shown in the drawings. If the hands move back, then reverse the direction in which you revolve the watch.

18. Ghost Ring

Your wrists are tied with a string or rope. You display a ring, Figure 20, explaining that it belonged to a friendly ghost who left it as a gift. The spectator is asked to close his eyes so you can encourage the ghost to send the ring temporarily into the fourth dimension. The spectator closes his eyes. When he opens them, the ring is securely linked onto the string, Figure 21. All apparatus is ungimmicked.

Method: The ring should be the size of a bracelet, that is, large

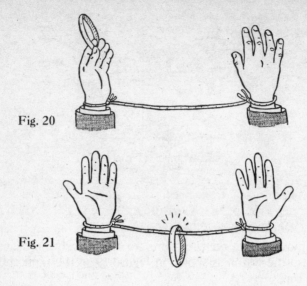

Fig. 20

Fig. 21

enough to slip over your wrist. A wooden or plastic bracelet is ideal.

Unknown to the spectator, you have two identical rings. One is slipped onto the wrist and is hidden inside the jacket or shirt sleeve. This preparation is done secretly. The other ring is the visible ring seen by the audience.

Have your wrists tied with string. Display the ring, Figure 20. Ask the spectator to close his eyes. When he does, slip the ring into your pocket. Slide the duplicate ring off your wrist and onto the center of the string. When the spectator opens his eyes, he sees the situation shown in Figure 21. Somehow, the ring seems to have become linked onto the string.

19. Behind That Door

If you wish to perform a trick like "Ghost Ring" (No. 18) at a party for several people, this version is just the ticket. One end of a long string is tied around your wrist. The other end is held by the spectator. Display a ring or bracelet as you step behind a door, Figure 22.

Remark that you have to step out of sight for a moment to summon a bashful ghost. He will help you put the ring through the fourth dimension.

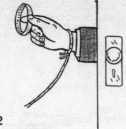

Fig. 22

When you step out from behind the door, the ring is linked onto the rope. The apparatus may be examined. There is no clue as to how the trick was accomplished.

Method: Unknown to the audience, you have two identical rings or bracelets. Slide one ring onto your wrist and push it up into your sleeve so it is concealed from view. This preparation is done secretly.

The string should be several feet long. Have one end tied to your wrist. The spectator holds the other end. Display the duplicate ring. Step behind the door. Let the audience have one last look at the ring, Figure 22. Then draw the hand out of sight behind the door.

Drop the ring into the pocket. Slide the other ring off the wrist and onto the rope. Then step out from behind the door to show the ring linked onto the string. If you can find adhesive labels or stickers, you can add a convincing touch to the trick. Place an adhesive sticker on the ring the audience sees. Ask someone to write his initials on the sticker. When you step behind the door, peel the sticker off the ring. Hide the ring in your pocket. Bring the other ring out of the sleeve and slide it onto the string. Then put the sticker on this ring.

When you step out into view, the audience sees the ring on the string and you can have the spectator verify that the initials are his.

20. Loopy Loop

"Loopy Loop" is a clever trick that uses nothing more than a piece of string. Carry a string in your pocket and you are always ready to perform this mystery. The spectator sees you tie the

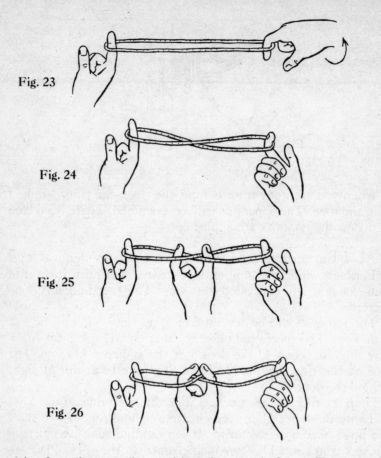

Fig. 23

Fig. 24

Fig. 25

Fig. 26

ends of a string together and loop it over his finger, Figure 23. It is impossible to get the string off without lifting it from his finger, but that is exactly what you accomplish.

Method: Use a piece of string about 60″ long. Tie the ends together. Loop the string over the spectator's finger. Your first finger (right hand) is pointed downward as shown in Figure 23.

Turn your hand in the direction of the arrow shown in Figure 23. Your finger now points upward, Figure 24, and the string is crossed in the middle.

Place your left first finger on one side of the crossing point, your left thumb on the other, Figure 25. Pinch the thumb and first finger of each hand together, Figure 26. This is just a precaution to keep the strands from getting tangled during the next move.

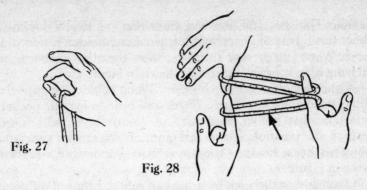

Fig. 27

Fig. 28

Turn the right hand palm down. Allow the string to fall so that it is now looped around the thumb, Figure 27.

Bring the right hand over to the spectator's hand. Place your thumb against his finger, Figure 28. As you do, say, "Now this locks the string in place. It is impossible to get it off."

Separate the left thumb and first finger. Slip the left first finger out from the strands. Grasp the strand that loops around the spectator's first finger. This strand is shown by the arrow in Figure 28. Say, "I'm going to try to get the string off your finger. Please close your eyes so we have an interval of darkness." When the spectator closes his eyes, gently tug on the string. It will slip free of his finger.

21. Band It

This is a new and different approach to the trick in which a rubber band ends up on your fingers in a magical manner. The spectator sees you loop a rubber band over your pinkie, Figure 29. The spectator then grasps your second and third fingers. Explain that you need a moment of darkness to work your magic.

The spectator closes his eyes. When he opens them he will be surprised to see that, even though he has held your fingers, the rubber band is now looped over your second and third fingers, Figure 30.

Fig. 29   Fig. 30

Method: The spectator does not know that you have a duplicate rubber band. It is slid over your left wrist and hidden inside your sleeve. When you present the trick, show the other rubber band and hang it on your little finger as shown in Figure 29.

Ask the spectator to close his eyes. When he does, remove the rubber band from your little finger and hide it in your pocket. Slide the other rubber band out from your sleeve and bring it down to the position shown in Figure 30. When the spectator opens his eyes, he sees the apparently impossible situation shown in Figure 30.

You can add to the trick by using two rubber bands of different colors. The spectator sees you hang a red and a green rubber band on your little finger. He picks a color, say red. Then he closes his eyes. When he opens them, the red rubber band is looped onto your middle fingers, even though he has held your fingers throughout.

The secret is that you have a duplicate red band and green band on your wrist, concealed in your sleeve. Whatever color the spectator picks, remove that band from your pinkie and hide it in your pocket. Remove the band of the same color from your wrist and slide it into position over your two middle fingers.

22. Interval of Darkness

If you wish to perform a trick like "Band It" on an impromptu basis, this version can be performed at a moment's notice. In this routine you place a rubber band on your first finger. The spectator grasps your finger as shown in Figure 31, thus trapping the rubber band. You say, "We will need an interval of darkness, so let's both close our eyes." You both close your eyes. When you open them a moment later, the rubber band is off your finger, Figure 32.

Fig. 31

Fig. 32

Ask the spectator to place the rubber band back, and then grasp your finger again. You have returned to the situation of Figure 31. Say, "It's harder to get a rubber band *on* my finger, but I'd like to give it a try."

Display a second rubber band. Both you and the spectator close your eyes. When you open them, the second band is on your finger.

Method: All you need to perform this mystery are a few rubber bands. They must be identical to one another. Once you are familiar with the secret, you may wish to try it with other objects like hoop-type bracelets. You should be wearing a jacket or long-sleeved shirt. The rubber bands are in your right pocket.

Withdraw a rubber band from your pocket. Place it on your left first finger. Ask the spectator to grasp your finger as in Figure 31. Say, "We will need a moment of darkness. Let's close our eyes." Close your eyes, wait a moment, then open them. (The spectator's eyes remain closed.) Silently slide the rubber band into your left sleeve so it is concealed from view.

Withdraw another rubber band from your pocket. Have the spectator open his eyes. He sees the situation shown in Figure 32. You have apparently removed the rubber band from your finger while he was holding your finger—an impossible trick!

Place the rubber band on your first finger. Ask the spectator to grasp your finger again. You are back at the situation shown in Figure 31.

Remove another band from your pocket. Say, "It's much harder to get a rubber band *on* than it is to get it off. I think I can do it." The spectator closes his eyes. Close your eyes also but open them after a moment.

Silently drop the rubber band back into your pocket. Then withdraw the hidden band from your jacket sleeve and slide it over your first finger. When the spectator opens his eyes, he sees *two* rubber bands on your finger—another impossible trick!

Mental Magic

Mind-reading tricks fall into a special category. People tend to believe that extrasensory perception exists, so they will accept mind-reading magic as "real" magic. In these circumstances they will not look for sleight of hand or other trickery, so your task is that much easier.

Mind-reading tricks generally rely on simple methods. You must disguise this by making it seem difficult to focus in on someone's thoughts. Struggle a bit before you reveal the thought-of number or the chosen date—pause, change your mind, then pretend it is all becoming clear and go on with the revelation. In this way you will be given credit for exceptional powers.

23. Beyond Numbers

People are impressed when you can perform mind-reading tricks with objects borrowed in their home. Newspapers can be found in almost any home. In this trick, when you are at a friend's home, you can borrow a newspaper or magazine and reveal a word or sentence chosen by them.

Method: Before you begin the trick, you must glance through the newspaper, seemingly at random. It is best to do this when no one else is in the room. Open the paper to page 7 and memorize the first word of the first sentence at the top of the page. If people are present, continue leafing through the paper, saying, "I want to be sure there are a lot of stories, but not too many ads to distract us. This paper looks fine."

Close the paper and place it before the spectator. Hand him a pencil and paper. Then turn your back.

"I'd like to try an experiment in numerology. Think of a day of the month like the fifth or the twelfth or the twenty-third. It could be the day of a friend's birthday, or the day when you expect to get a letter, or just a random number."

We will assume the spectator picks 14 and will carry through the example with this number. Tell the spectator:

1. Add 10 to your number: $14 + 10 = 24.$
2. Multiply this number by 2: $24 \times 2 = 48.$
3. Subtract 6: $48 - 6 = 42.$
4. Divide this number by 2: $42 \div 2 = 21.$
5. Subtract your original number: $21 - 14 = 7.$

This new number 7 seems to be a random number. Ask the spectator to open the newspaper to page 7 and look at the top line. With your back turned, you reveal the words, simply telling him the words you memorized earlier.

As performed above, the spectator will always arrive at the number 7, no matter what number he started with. If you wish to repeat the trick with a different outcome, in Step 3 ask the spectator to subtract 4 (instead of 6). He will arrive at 8 as the final number.

The trick can be performed with textbooks, astrology books, a school yearbook or any printed material to which you can attach an interesting story line.

24. Devil's Dictionary

Holding a dictionary so the pages face the spectator, you riffle through the pages until he calls stop. He is asked to remember the last word on the page. This is a random word that cannot be known in advance.

Closing the dictionary, you place one hand on it, concentrate for a moment and then reveal the chosen word. The dictionary may be borrowed. The trick can be repeated with different spectators.

Method: The trick can be done with any dictionary, but a paperback dictionary is easier to handle than one that is full size. Hold it as shown in Figure 33, with the dictionary facing the spectator. Turn your head aside and riffle the pages off the left thumb until the spectator calls stop.

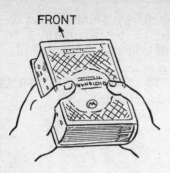

FRONT

Fig. 33

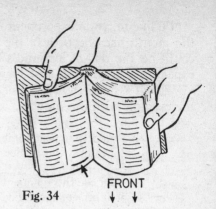

Fig. 34

FRONT

Same as last word
on page

Fig. 35

Hold the dictionary up so the spectator gets a clear view of the page. Ask him to remember the last entry on the page, that is, the word on the bottom right column for which a definition is given, Figure 34.

Unknown or unnoticed by most people is the fact that the last entry on the page is printed at the top of the page in bold letters, Figure 35. Glance at this word when you are about to close the dictionary and you know the spectator's selection. Repeat the process with a second spectator. Remember his word. Then go on to reveal each word.

You can make it dramatic by doing it a letter at a time, i.e., "I see a strong word, one that is used by the military. There is an O in it, two M's, a C and—yes, it's clear now. The word is 'COMMAND'."

25. Knowing the Future

Here is a mind-reading trick that can be performed in the living room or on the stage. Based on a classic trick using specially pre-

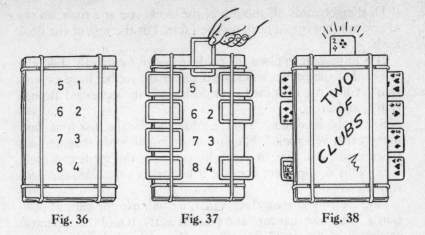

| Fig. 36 | Fig. 37 | Fig. 38 |

pared cards, this new version uses ordinary cards to achieve an effect very much like that which a real mind-reader would accomplish.

It uses a large piece of cardboard or a writing pad like the sketch pads used by artists. Four rubber bands are snapped around the edges, Figure 36. Eight playing cards are then slipped under the rubber bands. One of these cards is then freely chosen and placed at the top, Figure 37.

When the pad is turned around, there, in large letters, is the correct prediction of the card that would be chosen, Figure 38.

Method: The cardboard or sketch pad should measure at least $8^{1}/_{2}'' \times 11''$ so there will be enough room to place the eight cards. Snap rubber bands around the edges. On one side write the numbers 1 through 8 as shown in Figure 36. Turn the pad over and write the name of the card you wish to predict. In our example it will be the ♣2. Write "Two of Clubs" in large, clear letters.

Secretly place the prediction card (♣2 in our example) at a position ninth from the top of the deck. This completes the preparation.

To present the trick, display the apparatus so the audience can see the front of it, Figure 36. Remark that you have written a prediction, which is on the back. Explain that you want to use eight cards. Ask a spectator to remove from one to eight cards from the top of the deck. Turn your head aside while he does this, so you do not know the number of cards removed. Ask him to check that he has no more than eight cards.

Deal eight cards off the top of the deck, one at a time, on top of one another into a heap on the table. Put the rest of the deck aside.

It is important to place the cards in position correctly. Take the top card of the packet and slide it under the rubber band at position 1. Slide the next card in at position 2, the next card at position 3, and so on.

Say to the spectator, "Tell the audience, for the first time, how many cards you took." The spectator might reply that he took three cards. Ask him to check by counting the cards one more time. This is important because if he makes a mistake, the trick will not work.

Say, "Since you took three cards, we will use the card at position 3." Remove that card and place it at the top of the apparatus as shown in Figure 37. Do this slowly so the audience is aware you are not switching cards.

"Remember I said that I wrote a prediction before we began. For the first time we will see what card you chose and what card I predicted."

Turn the apparatus around, Figure 38. Point to the chosen card, and then to your prediction as you say, "You chose the two of clubs and I predicted you would pick the two of clubs. Thank you very much!"

26. Ribbon Revealed

Display three ribbons of different colors. Place them on the table and turn your back. Ask someone to hand you one of the ribbons behind your back. He is to hide the other ribbons. You turn and face the audience. Although the ribbon is out of sight behind your back, you are able to identify the color correctly. The trick may be repeated.

Method: Start with three ribbons of different colors, say red, white and blue. Each ribbon is 18″ long.

Clip one end of the red ribbon under your thumb. Let the ribbon hang over the back of the hand as shown in Figure 39. This will be the starting point for the preparation of each ribbon.

Wind the ribbon around the hand until you are near the end of the ribbon. Then trim end *B* so that it is even with end *A*, Figure 40. Unwind this ribbon from the hand and place it aside.

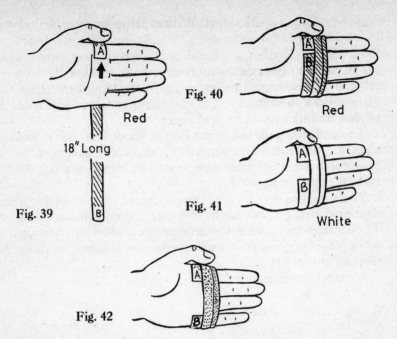

Fig. 39
18" Long
Red
A
B

Fig. 40
Red

Fig. 41
White

Fig. 42

Clip the white ribbon under the thumb exactly as shown in Figure 39. Wind the ribbon around the hand until you are near the end of the ribbon. Trim end B so that it is about 2″ from end A, Figure 41.

Clip the blue ribbon under the thumb as shown in Figure 39. Wind it around the hand until you are near the end of the ribbon. Trim end B so that it is 3″–4″ from end A, Figure 42.

To present the trick, show the three ribbons and drop them into a paper bag. Explain that they belong to a friend who is a medium and has trained them to give off thought waves about their identity. Turn your back. Ask a spectator to reach into the bag, remove a ribbon and hand it to you behind your back. Then ask him to put the bag aside.

Turn and face the audience. Keep the ribbon behind your back. Clip it under your thumb as shown in Figure 39 and wind it around your hand. As you do, say, "I'd like you to think of the color. Okay, I think I've got it. Now I'll read the mind of the ribbon and see if I get the same thought pattern."

As you speak, wind the ribbon around your hand. If the ends meet, it is the red ribbon. If there is a gap or space between the ends, it is the white ribbon. If there is a large gap between the ends, it is the blue ribbon.

27. Red, White, Blue

"Red, White, Blue" is a colorful prediction. It uses inexpensive props that can be seen by audiences large and small. On your table are three large envelopes. Each envelope leans against a glass or book so each envelope stands upright. Explain that each envelope contains *two* pieces of paper.

The audience sees you remove a red paper from the red envelope, Figure 43, a white paper from the white envelope, and a blue paper from the blue envelope. The papers are set out in front as shown in Figure 44.

The audience decides how the papers are to be moved around. The final arrangement might look like the one shown in Figure 45. Although this is a random arrangement, when you remove the other pieces of paper from each envelope, it is seen that your predictions are correct.

All apparatus is ordinary.

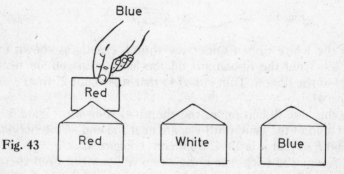

Fig. 43

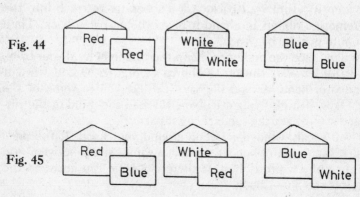

Fig. 44

Fig. 45

Method: Colorful envelopes and construction paper may be obtained in stores that sell school supplies. If you want to present "Red, White, Blue" at a moment's notice and color props are not available, you can write the colors on the envelopes and papers as shown in Figure 46. Remember that the larger the props, the more visible they are.

The setup is this. Place a red and a white paper in the red envelope, a white and a blue paper in the white envelope, and a blue and a red paper in the blue envelope. Figure 46 shows the preparation.

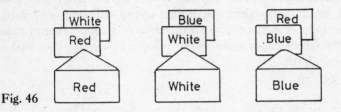

Fig. 46

When ready to present the trick, place three glasses on the table. Lean an envelope against each glass so the envelopes stand upright and can be clearly seen by the audience.

"This is the famous red, white and blue trick. It uses a red, a white and a blue envelope." Display the envelopes as shown in Figure 43. Jokingly add, "I wonder why it's called the red, white and blue trick."

After the envelopes are displayed, say, "In each envelope are *two* pieces of paper." Remove the red paper from the red envelope, the white paper from the white envelope, and the blue paper from the blue envelope. Place each paper in front of its envelope, Figure 44.

"I would like you to mix up the colors by placing a paper in front of an envelope of a *different* color. For example, you can place the red paper in front of either the white envelope or the blue envelope. You decide." Although it seems to the audience that there are many possible ways the papers can be arranged, in fact there are only two.

The audience might decide to place the red paper in front of the white envelope, the blue paper in front of the red envelope, and the white paper in front of the blue envelope.

When this arrangement has been decided on, the trick ends as follows. "The reason I call this the red, white and blue trick is because, even though you had a free choice, we *still* have red, white and blue in each case." Point out that you have a red envelope with a blue paper in front of it. Then remove the white paper from inside the envelope to show three different colors—red, white and blue.

Similarly, remove the blue paper from the second envelope to show three different colors. Finally, remove the red paper from the last envelope to show red, white and blue in that group also.

Sometimes the audience will arrive at the other arrangement. This is shown in Figure 47. You are set for this outcome also. Say, "Remember, I said I had *two* papers in each envelope when we started. You put the white paper next to the red envelope. Inside the envelope is a matching white piece of paper." Remove the matching white paper from the envelope. Show the envelope is otherwise empty.

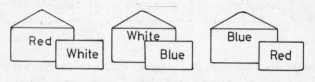

Fig. 47

There is a blue paper in front of the next envelope. Remove the matching blue paper from inside the envelope. Finally, point out that there is a red paper in front of the last envelope. Remove the matching red paper from this envelope to show a perfect match.

When doing the trick, be sure to show that, except for the second piece of paper, each envelope is otherwise empty. The apparatus may be left with the audience at the finish.

Paper Magic

Tricks with paper have many advantages. The apparatus is inexpensive. It is lightweight and packs flat. Best of all, if you use construction paper of different colors, the apparatus is showy and colorful. The tricks in this chapter use apparatus ranging from paper bags to paper cups to paper rings.

28. The Paper Rabbit

Magicians are expected to produce rabbits. If you have a sheet of paper handy, you can quickly create a rabbit with a few tucks and snips.

The paper can be any size, but a square of white paper 8″ on a side is about right, Figure 48. Fold it in half, Figure 49. Then fold the top down to form the triangular piece shown in Figure 50.

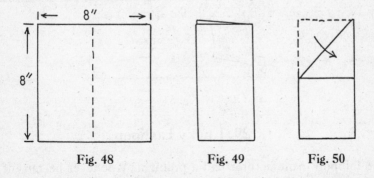

Fig. 48   Fig. 49   Fig. 50

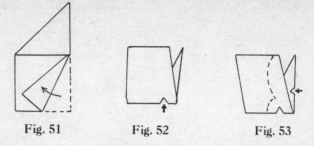

Fig. 51   Fig. 52   Fig. 53

Fold the bottom over to form another triangle, Figure 51. Then fold the bottom half up so it is even with the top half, Figure 52.

Cut a notch in the folded paper as shown by the arrow in Figure 52.

Open the paper out a bit and cut another notch in the back portion as shown by the arrow in Figure 53. Then cut along the dotted lines shown in Figure 53.

Carefully open out the paper and you will have the rabbit shown in Figure 54. It may be necessary to trim the ears a bit to shape them properly. Prop the paper rabbit up against a glass or book so he can watch things while you do your magic act.

If you have construction paper of different colors handy, you can make several rabbits and hand them out to people who help you during the course of your performance.

Fig. 54

29. Lucky Lollipop

A lollipop manufacturer had a problem. Whenever he ran off a batch, one would have a lollipop at each end of the stick. The sit-

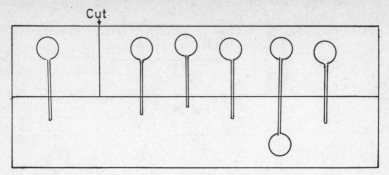

Fig. 55

uation is shown in Figure 55. The double lollipop is the second from the right.

Calling attention to the fact that there are six lollipops in a batch, you perform a bit of magic to set things right. In the process, the six lollipops magically increase to seven.

Method: Use a piece of paper 8″ long and 3″ wide. Draw a line across the middle. Then divide the line into 1″ segments.

Draw a lollipop 1″ from the left, then another 3″ from the left, then four more at 1″ intervals. The lollipop second from the right is a double. The six lollipops are shown in Figure 55.

Cut the paper at a point 2″ from the left, making the cut from the top down to the middle. Then cut the paper from left to right across the middle. The cut lines are also shown in Figure 55.

Show the six lollipops as indicated in Figure 55. Point out that the one second from the right has a lollipop at each end of the stick.

You are going to rearrange the pieces of paper as follows. The starting position is shown in Figure 56. To make six lollipops into seven, bring piece *A* down to the right and *B* down to the left. This new position is shown in Figure 57. Then bring the long

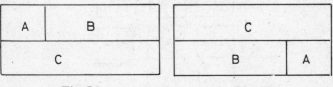

Fig. 56   Fig. 57

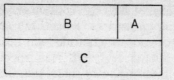

Fig. 58

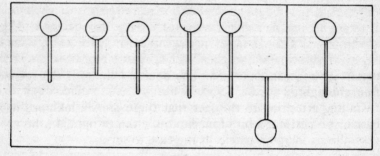

Fig. 59

piece *C* down below the other pieces to the position shown in Figure 58.

The result is shown in Figure 59. The double lollipop no longer exists and you now have seven lollipops.

30. Boys and Girls

The audience sees you write boys' and girls' names on a square of paper. The names are alternated so there is a boy's name at the upper left, a girl's name next to it, then a boy's name, a girl's name, and so on, until you have written nine names. The paper is torn as shown in Figure 60.

The nine torn pieces are dropped into a hat or box. Someone

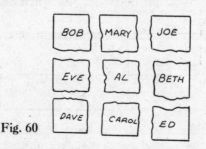

Fig. 60

from the audience shakes the contents of the box so the names are well mixed.

Keeping your head turned aside, you reach in and take a piece of paper in each hand, Figure 61. The spectator is asked to guess which hand contains a boy's name. He might guess the left hand. You open that hand and allow him to take that piece of paper. He is correct; the paper does contain a boy's name.

The piece of paper not picked is tossed back into the box. You then pick two new pieces of paper and ask the spectator to guess which is a girl's name. Once again he is correct. The trick is repeated several more times. The spectator is always correct.

Method: The secret is simple but well concealed. Look at the torn pieces of paper shown in Figure 60. The slips with the girls' names all have *one* smooth edge. All of the other slips have boys' names.

When you reach into the box the first time, you can locate two slips with boys' names by sense of touch because these slips either have two smooth edges or (as in the case of the "Al" slip in the center in Figure 60) no smooth edges. Take one in each hand. Close the hands into fists and bring them out into view, Figure 61.

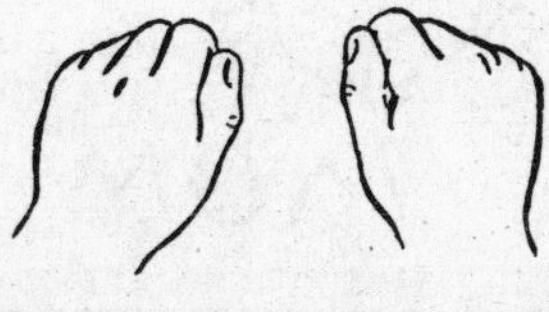

Fig. 61

Whichever hand the spectator chooses, that hand will contain a paper with a boy's name. Toss the unselected slip back into the box.

The next time, take a slip with a girl's name in each hand. This is done by sense of touch also; just pick two slips, each of which has one smooth edge.

Proceed in the same way three or four more times. Each time the spectator is correct.

31. WOW! MOM!

Hand the spectator two pictures like the ones shown in Figure 62. While you turn your back the spectator chooses either one.

Even though your back is turned, you write something on a piece of paper that proves to be the word chosen by the spectator. No questions are asked, and the trick may be done any time.

Method: Draw pictures like the ones in Figure 62, one on each of two pieces of paper. Both words must be spelled in capital letters. The papers should be the same size. Have the spectator hold the WOW paper in his right hand and the MOM paper in his left hand.

Fig. 62

Pick up a pad and a pencil. Turn your back to the spectator. Ask him to decide on one paper and hold it to his forehead to better concentrate.

With your back still to the spectator, print WOW on the pad in large letters. Say, "I think I've got it. You can lower your hand now."

Turn and face the spectator. Glance at his hands. Because he raised one hand to his forehead, the back of that hand will look pale compared to the other hand. The reason is that the blood drained from the hand when it was raised.

If the spectator's right hand looks pale, you know he chose the WOW card. Hold the pad so the writing is right side up. Turn it so the spectator sees that you wrote the word "WOW." Say, "Your word, right?"

If his left hand looks pale compared to his right hand, he chose the word "MOM." Turn the pad around and hold it up so the writing spells "MOM." Say, "I'm positive you chose the word 'MOM'. Right?" He must agree.

32. Out of Nowhere

If you plan to do a show at a birthday party, it is a good idea to produce a gift for the birthday child in a magical manner. This is an inexpensive method that allows you to produce anything that can fit into a ten-ounce cup. It is used here to produce a toy car.

Method: You will need three ten-ounce paper cups. Larger cups may be used to produce larger objects. Cut the bottom from one cup, Figure 63. Nest this bottomless cup in another cup, Figure 64. Turn the double cup over so it is mouth down on the table. Stand the third cup on top of it.

You will also need a paper tube that acts as a cover. A few sheets of plain white paper or a sheet of construction paper may be used. They are taped together to form a tube like the one shown in Figure 65. The tube should be of such a size as to fit easily over the cups.

Beforehand, put a toy car in the top cup. Lower the paper tube over the apparatus, Figure 66. The audience is unaware of this

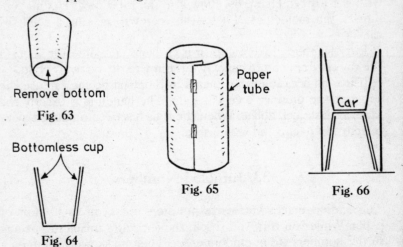

Remove bottom

Fig. 63

Bottomless cup

Fig. 64

Paper tube

Fig. 65

Car

Fig. 66

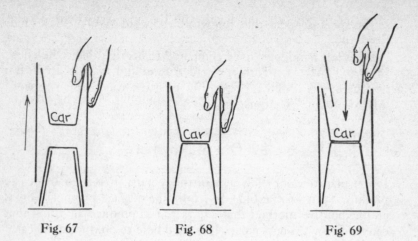

| Fig. 67 | Fig. 68 | Fig. 69 |

preparation. The apparatus may be kept on a tray and carried to the performance area set up as described here.

To perform, grasp the cup with the toy car and the paper tube. Lift them up, revealing the double cup, Figure 67.

With the other hand, pick up the double cup. Say, "I brought two cups with me." Show the double cup all around and set it, mouth up, on the table. Lift out the inner (bottomless) cup and set it on the table. Pick up the ordinary empty cup, turn it mouth down and rest it on the table. Lower the tube over it, Figure 68. Unknown to the audience, the cup with the toy car now rests on top of the empty cup.

Pick up the bottomless cup and slowly lower it into the cup with the toy car, Figure 69. Blow into the tube. Say, "Hot air condenses the molecules. That's the secret to making a good toy car."

Lift the tube. Take a cup in each hand and slide (or "pour") the toy car from cup to cup. Give the toy to the birthday child.

If it is an occasion other than a birthday party, you can use the apparatus to produce a cup of soda. The handling is exactly the same as described above. When the soda has been produced, pour it from cup to cup and set it aside.

33. Jumbled Numbers

The audience sees you write numbers on seven small slips of paper. While you turn your back, the spectator mixes the papers so the numbers are in random order. Then he skewers them on a safety pin, Figure 70, and hands you the apparatus behind your back.

The papers are behind your back, so you cannot see them. You tear them from the safety pin one at a time and place them on the table in a row, number side down.

The spectator is asked for his phone number. When he gives it to you, you turn over the papers one at a time. The numbers have been arranged so they they exactly match the spectator's phone number!

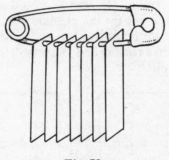

Fig. 70

Method: You must know the spectator's phone number ahead of time. Write it down, one digit on each of seven slips of paper. Arrange the papers in correct order and push a safety pin through them. When you are ready to perform the trick, secretly fasten this pin to your shirt in back. Then put on a jacket to cover the apparatus.

Show the spectator seven blank pieces of paper and a duplicate pin. Jot down the numbers on these slips of paper. Mix them and hand them to the spectator. While you turn your back, he mixes them further and puts them on the safety pin. Take the pin behind your back and pin it under your jacket. Remove the second pin with the numbers in correct order.

Tear the slips off in correct order and place them, writing side down, on the table as you remark about your powers to see around corners.

Ask the spectator for his telephone number. He will be surprised when he sees that you have arranged the slips of paper so as to duplicate his telephone number exactly.

The trick can also be done with letters of the alphabet to spell the spectator's name, or with words which, when put in correct order, duplicate the opening line of a popular song.

34. Red Magic

Make up a sign in block letters by printing the word "TOMATO" with a red pen, "CELERY" with a black pen. Print the words vertically as shown in Figure 71.

Tell your friend that this particular red ink seems to contain a magical ingredient. Ask him to hold the sign up to a mirror. TOMATO will still read the same, but CELERY will be reversed.

You can make up other signs like the ones shown in Figure 71. On each sign the word on the left is printed in red ink, the word on the right in black ink (or ink of some other color). The black writing is reversed in the mirror; the red writing looks the same. In the next chapter, a trick called "Reverso" (No. 39) expands on this curious principle.

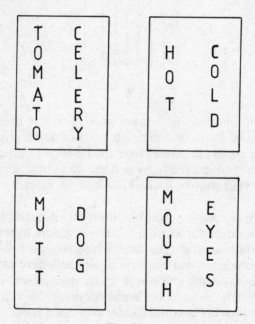

Fig. 71

35. The Rings of Saturn

"The planet Saturn is surrounded by mysterious rings. They don't act like rings on Earth. I made up a few samples to show you what I mean." You then show how mysterious the rings really are; when cut in half, they act in surprising ways.

Method: Cut four long strips from a newspaper. The strips should be as long as possible and about 2″ wide.

Glue or tape the ends of one strip together as shown in Figure 72. Put this paper aside.

Give one end of the next strip a twist and glue or tape the ends together, Figure 73. Prepare the next strip exactly the same way. Thus, you have two strips prepared as shown in Figure 73.

Prepare the last strip by giving it a double twist and gluing the ends together as shown in Figure 74.

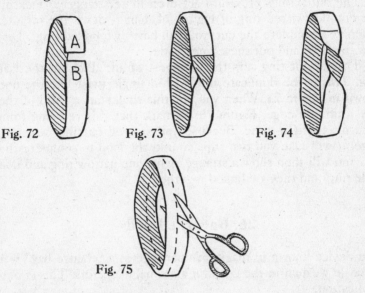

Fig. 72   Fig. 73   Fig. 74

Fig. 75

You want the strips of paper to be as long as possible because, when they are formed into rings as described above, the longer the strip of paper is, the better concealed the twists will be.

To present the trick, pick up the loop shown in Figure 72. Cut it down the middle as indicated by the dotted line in Figure 75. As you do, say, "This is the way a ring acts here on the planet Earth. When we cut it down the middle, we get two separate rings." When you complete the cut, hold one ring in each hand to show them separated. Then put them on the table.

Pick up the twisted ring shown in Figure 73 and cut it down the middle. As you do, say, "On Saturn, there are inner rings, outer rings and far-out rings. Here's an inner ring. When we cut it down the middle, it acts differently." When you complete the cut, you do not get two separate rings. You get one large ring. Display the large ring and place it aside.

Fig. 76

Start cut here

"The outer rings of Saturn act even more strangely." Pick up the double-twisted ring of Figure 74. Cut it down the middle. When you complete the cut, you will have two linked rings. Display the rings and put these rings aside.

"The far-out ring acts the strangest of all." Pick up the last ring. This is the duplicate ring with a single twist like the one shown in Figure 73. When you cut this ring, start a third of the way from one edge, Figure 76. Remark that this is a ring from Saturn's twilight zone. Because you started cutting near one edge, it will take you two trips around the loop to complete the cut. You will then show a strange sight, one narrow ring and one wide ring, and they are linked together.

36. Favorite Food

The device known in magician's parlance as a "change bag" is a versatile weapon in the conjuror's arsenal of secrets. This is one application.

Remark that your favorite food is pizza. The audience sees you write down three of your favorite kinds of pizza on three separate pieces of paper and drop them into a paper bag.

The spectator says that his favorites are cheeseburgers, fried rice and barbecued chicken. He writes the names of these favorite foods on three separate pieces of paper and drops them into the bag.

The bag is shaken to mix the contents. The spectator reaches in and picks three pieces of paper, which he hands to the magician. Then the spectator reaches in, removes the other three pieces of paper, and keeps them.

Amazingly enough, he has picked for the magician his three favorite kinds of pizza, and he has picked for himself the slips bearing the words "cheeseburger," "fried rice" and "barbecued chicken," his own favorite foods.

Method: The change bag is the secret behind this trick. It is easily made and can be used over and over again. You will need two identical paper bags. Cut the front panel from one and slide it into the inside of the other bag so the top of the panel is even with the top of the bag. Tape it to the center of the bottom of the bag, Figure 77, so that it divides the bag into two equal compartments.

Since this panel or flap is taped only to the bottom of the bag, it can be swung back and forth as shown in Figure 78, so that either compartment can be sealed off and the other compartment opened. This is the basic operating principle of the change bag; you can secretly change compartments.

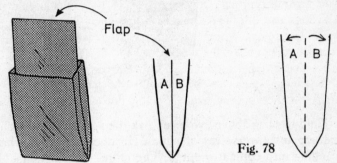

Flap

A B

Fig. 77

A B

Fig. 78

To prepare for this trick, write "pepperoni pizza" on one slip of paper, "extra-cheese pizza" on another, and "anchovy pizza" on a third. Place them in compartment *A* of the change bag. Leave the flap in the upright position of Figure 77. This preparation is done secretly.

When you are ready to perform the trick, remark that pizza is one of your favorite foods. Say that you will jot down three of your favorite kinds of pizza. On the top sheet of the pad write "meatball pizza," tear it off and drop it into compartment *A*. On the next sheet write "sausage pizza" and drop it into compartment *A*. On the third sheet write "onion pizza" and drop it in compartment *A*. Do not show the spectator what you have written. The bag should be off to one side so the spectator cannot look down inside.

Ask the spectator to write down three of his favorite foods, one on each of three sheets of paper. When he has done this, take the papers from him and drop them into compartment *B*.

Grasp the bag so that you can push the flap over toward the compartment *B* side, Figure 78. Hold the bag up so it is above eye level. The audience is thus prevented from seeing down inside the bag. Holding the bag between the hands, Figure 79, shake the contents back and forth so that the slips are well mixed.

Fig. 79

Hold the bag above eye level. Ask the spectator to reach in and remove any three slips of paper. He does not know that he is reaching into compartment *A*. Therefore, the only slips of paper he can take are those with different kinds of pizza written on them.

Take the three pieces of paper from him. As you pretend to shake the bag some more, move the flap over so that the compartment *B* side is open. Ask the spectator to remove the remaining three slips of paper and hold them. He will be amazed to discover that he correctly sorted things out so he got back *his* favorite food and you got back *yours*.

The trick can also be done with favorite television shows, favorite sports teams, favorite books and so on.

Novelty Magic

The tricks in this chapter are novelty routines that can be used to add something different to a magic act. They use offbeat props—everything from rings to socks to chairs—but they are easy to do and just the ticket when you want a change of pace from more traditional magic.

37. Vanishing Ring

"I borrow rings and other accessories from a friend of mine. He's a ghost, so when he wants something back, it disappears." As you speak, display a ring in the left hand. The right hand grasps a silk scarf as shown in Figure 80. The grip is important. The thumb and little finger are on the near side of the scarf; the first, second and third fingers are on the far side.

Bring the scarf to a position in front of the ring, so that the ring is hidden from audience view. Slip the right little finger into the ring as shown in Figure 81.

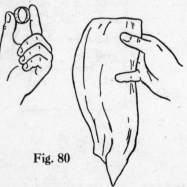

Fig. 80

Fig. 81

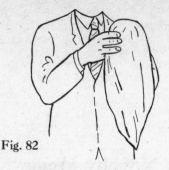

Fig. 82

Now bring the right hand back toward the body. Allow the ring to fall into the left shirt or jacket pocket. The audience view is shown in Figure 82. The scarf hides the secret move.

Move the left hand forward until it slides out from under the scarf. Show the left hand to be empty. Then shake out the scarf. The ring has vanished.

38. Hank the Ghost

"I was visited by a ghost named Henry. I call him Hank. He left behind a sock. I have two here on the table, one white and one blue. Can you tell which one is Hank's sock?"

The spectator might guess the blue one. "If the blue one belongs to Hank the ghost, it should act in a ghostly fashion." The audience sees you display a large cloth as shown in Figure 83. You then cross your arms as you cover the apparatus, Figure 84. When you straighten out your arms, the blue sock has indeed acted in ghostly fashion; it is now inside the glass, Figure 85.

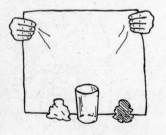

Fig. 83

Fig. 84

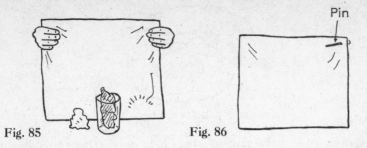

Fig. 85   Fig. 86

Method: The cloth can be any large scarf. A towel or short-sleeved shirt may even be substituted in a pinch. Just make sure the material is thick enough to prevent people from seeing through it, and that the cloth is large enough to cover the props. The only preparation is to insert a straight pin through the upper right corner, Figure 86.

When ready to present the trick, place two socks of different colors on the table with the glass. Socks are funny items of apparatus and add a touch of humor to the trick. If they are not available, you may use handkerchiefs or other similar objects. Just make sure they are of a soft material so they will not make noise when secretly placed into the glass.

Display the cloth as shown in Figure 83. The left hand then brings its end of the cloth around in front of the apparatus, while the right hand moves to the left. When the arms are crossed, stick the pin into the left shoulder of your jacket, Figure 87, making sure you do not stick yourself.

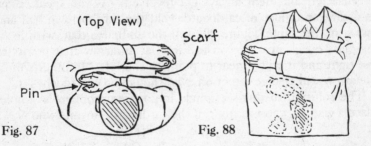

Fig. 87   Fig. 88

This end of the cloth is now anchored in place. The right hand secretly picks up the chosen sock and stuffs it into the glass, Figure 88. Keep the right arm pressed to the side so there is no arm movement visible to the audience. As you perform the secret action, remark that Hank's sock needs a moment of privacy to act in ghostly fashion.

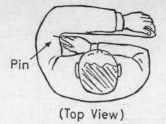

Fig. 89 (Top View)

Grasp the right end of the cloth with the right hand. Straighten the arms, bringing the cloth behind the apparatus once again. The audience sees the situation of Figure 85. The chosen sock has mysteriously jumped into the glass.

Practice to get the moves down smoothly. Make sure you wear a jacket, and not a shirt or sweater, when doing the trick. This makes it easier to stick the pin into the fabric and have it stay in place. You may wish to try sticking the pin into the left jacket sleeve (rather than the shoulder) as shown in Figure 89. With this approach, the right hand moves directly to the left, rather than back toward the body. Try each method and pick the one that works best for you.

39. Reverso

"In Looking-Glass Land, everything is the opposite. A right-handed person would be left-handed in Looking-Glass Land because left and right always get reversed." As you speak, draw an arrow on a piece of cardboard. Fold the cardboard in half and rest it on the table, Figure 90. Tell the audience that, with looking-glass eyeglasses on, you can look at an arrow that points to the right and it will appear to point to the left. "In other words, the arrow will change direction even though no one touches it."

The solution to this seemingly impossible problem is simple. Place a glass of water in front of the cardboard. Anyone who views

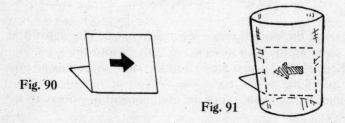

Fig. 90

Fig. 91

the arrow through the water will be surprised to discover that it has changed direction, Figure 91.

There are many ways this strange principle can be explored. For example, write 08010 on a piece of cardboard, Figure 92. Remark that in Looking-Glass Land, numbers have a way of suddenly changing places.

Point out that the 8 is on the left and the 1 on the right of center. Then put a glass of water in front of the numbers. When viewed through the water, the 8 and the 1 have mysteriously changed places, Figure 93.

It also works with words made from the capital letters A-H-I-M-O-T-U-V-W-X-Y. For example, write "YAM" in block letters on a piece of cardboard, Figure 94. When viewed through the glass of water, the Y and the M change places to produce the word "MAY."

Make sure the writing is bold and clear. The glass should be a straight-sided clear glass for best results.

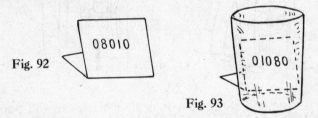

Fig. 92

Fig. 93

Fig. 94

40. Chair Lift

Place a chair against the wall. Put a book on top of it. Ask a boy to stand facing the chair, lift the chair and then straighten up. It seems a simple task but he will find it impossible to do.

You then place a second book on the chair, thus increasing the weight. Ask a girl to lift the chair and then straighten up. Even though there is increased weight on the chair due to the added book, she does it easily.

This is a good stunt to do at a party because most boys cannot do it while most girls can do it with ease.

Method: Use a chair without armrests. Place it sidewise to the wall, about an inch from the wall. Put a paperback book on the chair. Ask a boy to stand facing the chair, his feet lined up with the chair legs and about an inch from them.

Ask him to grasp the chair as shown in Figure 95, and to lean over so his head is resting against the wall. Say to him, "Can you lift the chair off the floor?" Be certain his head remains in contact with the wall. He should have no trouble lifting the chair, Figure 96. Then say, "Can you straighten yourself up while still holding the chair?" He will find it impossible.

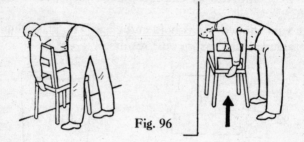

Fig. 95   Fig. 96

Some people will think that it is all a matter of the person being off-balance, but the explanation is different. Thank him for his participation. Place a second paperback book on the chair. "We'll just add a little more weight," you say. Then ask a girl to help you out. She follows the same procedure, but with a much different outcome. When asked to lift the chair and then straighten up, she does it easily! It is a curious fact of science that most boys cannot straighten up but most girls can!

41. Raise Your Foot

At a party you can demonstrate something that is impossible for your friends to do, but which you can do with ease. Ask someone to stand in a doorway so that his right arm and his right foot are against the doorjamb, Figure 97. Now ask him to raise his left foot slowly in the air. He cannot do it without falling over.

Invite several people to try it. It looks simple until it is tried; only then does the impossibility of the task become clear. When

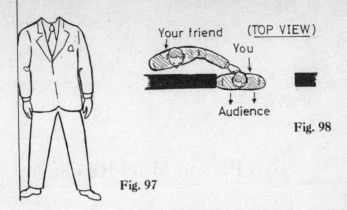

Fig. 97

Fig. 98

everyone has given up, step to the doorway and stand as shown in Figure 97. Remark that you have studied the secrets of the East and can levitate the left half of your body just enough to perform the demonstration.

Unknown to your audience, you have a friend who quietly walks up to the other side of the doorway, Figure 98. He grasps your belt and holds on while you slowly lift your left foot. The people in the room cannot see your friend, so it appears as if you have done the impossible. Have your friend sneak off to another room as you walk away from the doorway.

Invite others to try again. Explain that it helps if they think in terms of levitation, floating, becoming lighter than air, and so on. Having seen your success, they will be encouraged to give it another try. It is impossible for anyone to lift his foot when standing as shown in Figure 97.

Two-Person Mind Reading

Two-person tricks are a special area of mind reading. In the two-person trick, the magician introduces his assistant as someone who is adept at tuning in on the thoughts of others. Many people believe that two-person communication by thought waves is possible (it would certainly cut down on phone bills). Experiments in psychic communication have gone on for decades. The tricks in this chapter show what it would look like if it proved to be true.

As in all other areas of mind reading, do not make the trick look too easy. Your assistant should hesitate, get a word or two wrong, correct herself, then go on to reveal the correct information. This heightens suspense and makes the trick seem harder than it really is. You will enjoy that much more praise from your audience as a result.

42. Truth in Labeling

In magic parlance, a *medium* is a magician's assistant, traditionally a woman, who helps in the performance of mindreading tricks. In this demonstration, the medium goes into an adjoining room. The magician places four bottles of soda on the table, each with a straw, Figure 99.

Someone in the audience chooses a bottle of soda and takes a sip. The medium comes back into the room and immediately announces which bottle was chosen.

The trick may be repeated under tighter conditions. The medium is first blindfolded and taken to an adjoining room. The door is closed. Someone from the audience steps forward and takes a sip from any bottle. The blindfolded medium is led back

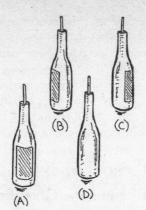

Fig. 99

into the room. Once again she correctly reveals which soda was chosen.

No questions are asked and no words spoken until the medium reveals the correct information. There are no gimmicks. Borrowed articles may be used.

Method: In Figure 99, notice that the bottles of soda are placed on the table so that the labels point in different directions. The label on bottle *A* points straight ahead; the label on bottle *B* points to the left; the label on *C* points to the right; the label on *D* points away from you.

When a spectator steps forward and takes a sip from a bottle of soda, stand so that you face in the same direction as the label on the chosen bottle. Thus, if bottle *B* was chosen, you would face in the direction shown in Figure 100. When the medium enters the room, she glances at you, sees in which direction you are facing and picks the bottle whose label faces the same direction. Of course she cannot make it seem too obvious; she should not look directly at you, but rather take a glimpse out of the corner of her eye.

Fig. 100

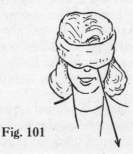

Fig. 101

If she is blindfolded, the method is almost the same. When the medium enters the room, she glances down the blindfold, Figure 101. Of course she cannot see which way you are facing, but she does not have to; she looks at your shoes and sees which way *they* are pointing. The label on the chosen bottle points in the same direction.

She is then led to the table and stands in front of it. Again looking down the blindfold, she is able to look at each bottle and quickly find the correct one.

43. Reading the Classifieds

On your table are several crumpled ads from the local newspaper, Figure 102. A spectator mixes them and chooses one. The chosen ad is opened and placed on a pad.

You draw three lines on the pad, Figure 103. Ask the spectator to pick three random words from the ad and jot them down in

Fig. 102

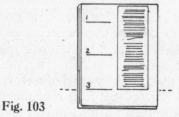

Fig. 103

the spaces on the pad. He can pick common words like "the" or less common words. The choice is entirely his to make. After he has written three words, he hides the ad.

The medium is in the next room. She is given the pad and pencil. For a moment she studies the three chosen words. Then she correctly identifies the ad hidden in the spectator's pocket.

Method: There is no verbal communication between you and the medium. She gets all the necessary information from what is written on the pad. Each ad is a different size, Figure 104. Crum-

Fig. 104

ple them and place them on the table as shown in Figure 102. Invite the medium to enter an adjoining room and close the door.

Ask a spectator to mix the ads and choose one. Open out the chosen ad and place it on the pad so the top of the ad lines up with the top of the pad, Figure 103. Draw three lines. The positions of the first two lines do not matter, but the position of the third line is important. As shown in Figure 103, it is drawn at the bottom of the ad. This will later tell the medium how long that classified ad is.

Ask the spectator to choose any three words from the ad and jot them down in the numbered spaces on the pad. Then he hides the ad.

Someone brings the pad and pencil to your assistant in the next room. You have previously given her a duplicate set of ads from another copy of that same day's newspaper. Another way to supply her with copies is to cut out the desired ads and run off copies on a duplicating machine.

When she is alone in the next room, the medium matches the length indicated on the pad with the ad of the same length in her possession. Then she goes on to reveal to the audience the general content of the chosen ad.

44. Behind Closed Doors

In this trick, your medium goes into an adjoining room and closes the door. Someone removes a coin from his pocket and seals it in an envelope along with three or four other coins. Without asking a question, the medium reveals the chosen coin.

Method: Your assistant enters an adjoining room and closes the door. It will seem to the audience that the door has been closed to isolate the medium, but the closed door figures into the method. Ask the spectator to remove three or four coins from his pocket and place them on the table. Have him choose one coin by holding it up so the rest of the audience can see it.

Hand him an envelope. He is requested to seal all the coins inside the envelope.

Take the envelope from him and slide it under the door. If the chosen coin is a penny, slide the envelope under the door at the far left. If it is a nickel, slide it under the door just left of center. If it is a dime, slide it under the door just to the right of center. If the chosen coin is a quarter, slide it under the door at the far right. This system tells the medium which coin was chosen. It is summarized in Figure 105.

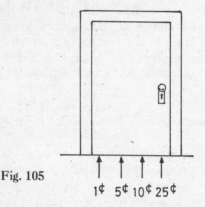

Fig. 105

1¢ 5¢ 10¢ 25¢

As soon as the envelope is slid under the door, the medium knows the chosen coin. She takes the envelope, shakes it, then slowly reveals the chosen coin. When the envelope is returned to the spectator, he sees that it is still sealed.

45. Behind Closed Doors II

If asked to repeat the previous trick, you can switch to a different method. In this case the spectator seals the coins in the envelope and hands the envelope directly to the medium. A code seems out of the question, but a code is indeed used.

Method: Type up four envelopes like the ones shown in Figure 106. You would put your name and address in the center of each envelope. The envelopes all look the same, but there are small differences among them. Envelope *A* is used to tell the

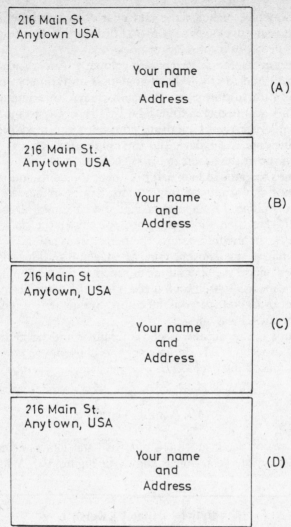

(A)

216 Main St
Anytown USA

Your name
and
Address

216 Main St.
Anytown USA

Your name
and
Address

(B)

216 Main St
Anytown, USA

Your name
and
Address

(C)

216 Main St.
Anytown, USA

Your name
and
Address

(D)

Fig. 106

medium that the chosen coin is a penny. There is no period after "St" and no comma after "Anytown."

Envelope *B* is used to tell the medium a nickel was chosen. There is a period after "St" but no comma after "Anytown."

Envelope *C* tells the medium a dime was chosen. There is no period after "St" but there is a comma after "Anytown."

Envelope *D* is used to tell the medium that a quarter was chosen. There is a period after "St" and a comma after "Anytown."

Place a penny, nickel, dime and quarter in envelope *A*. Then stack the four envelopes in *A-B-C-D* order, with A on top. Place the four envelopes in your jacket pocket.

To present the trick, remove envelope *A*. Ask a spectator to look it over and satisfy himself that it is an ordinary envelope. Then ask him to dump out the coins. Say, "In a moment I'm going to ask you to pick a coin. First I'd like my assistant to leave the room." When your medium goes into the next room and closes the door, take back the envelope and place it in your pocket on top of the others.

Ask the spectator to look carefully over the coins and pick one that makes the strongest impression. Say he picks the penny. Remove envelope *A* from your pocket and have him place all four coins in it. He then slides the envelope under the door. Seeing envelope *A*, the medium knows the penny was chosen.

If the nickel was chosen, remove envelope *B*. This looks just like the envelope the spectator examined at the beginning, so he will not suspect a switch took place. Have the coins placed in his envelope and given to your medium. Seeing envelope *B*, she knows the nickel was chosen.

Similarly, if the dime was chosen, you would have the coins placed in envelope *C*. If the quarter was chosen, you would have the coins placed in envelope *D*.

46. Magic Mind

Nine pieces of paper are filled out with the names of common objects. A sample selection is shown in Figure 107. While your

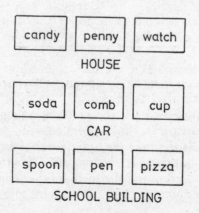

Fig. 107

medium turns her back, a spectator picks an object. Say he picks the candy in Figure 107.

Your medium asks two questions. The first question is, "Is the chosen object something I would find in a house, a car or a school building?"

You might reply, "A house."

Your medium says, "And if I was going to send it to a friend, would I put it in an envelope, a box or a bag?"

You reply, "An envelope."

The medium then says, "Oh, of course, the candy was chosen!"

The trick may be repeated one more time. The medium asks the same two questions and goes on to reveal the chosen object.

Method: This trick uses a spoken code to get the proper information to your assistant. The first group of three objects is associated with the word "house," the second group with the word "car," and the third group with the phrase "school building." This is shown in Figure 107.

If the spectator picks the candy, you know this is in the first group. When your assistant asks if the object could be found in a house, a car or a school building, you want to tell her, secretly, that the object is in the first group. Therefore, you pick the first word ("house") to indicate to her that the object is one of those in the first group of three. Your assistant now knows the chosen object was either the candy, the penny or the watch.

candy	penny	watch
(envelope)	(box)	(bag)

Fig. 108

When the medium asks if the chosen object could be mailed in an envelope, a box or a bag, you pick "envelope" to indicate that the chosen object is the first one in the chosen group. This part of the code is shown in Figure 108. The medium then goes to the table, picks up the first object in the first group, and says, "This is it."

To summarize, your answer to the first question tells your assistant which *group* of three objects contains the chosen object. Your answer to the second question tells her which *object* in that group is the chosen object.

Here is another example. Suppose the chosen object is the comb. This object is in the second group. When the medium asks

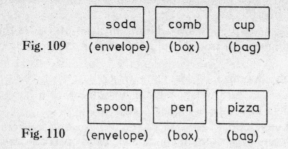

Fig. 109   soda (envelope)   comb (box)   cup (bag)

Fig. 110   spoon (envelope)   pen (box)   pizza (bag)

if the object can be found in the house, car or school, you pick the *second* word ("car") to indicate secretly to the medium that the object is in the *second* group. When the medium asks if the object should be mailed in an envelope, box or bag, you want to code that the chosen object is the second object in the group, so you pick the second choice ("box"). This part of the code is shown in Figure 109.

To take one more example, if the chosen object is "pizza," pick "school building" in answer to the first question, "bag" in answer to the second question, Figure 110. The trick may be repeated one more time.

47. Think Alike

You place nine or ten common items in a row on the table. These may be a coin, a cup, an envelope, a ruler, a pencil, a candy bar, etc. Your assistant looks them over and turns her back. She is then blindfolded.

A spectator now chooses one of the objects. He does this by picking up that object, showing it to the audience and putting it back. It does not have to go back to its original location.

Your medium says, "Hand me the first and second objects." She takes one in each hand, testing for mental vibrations from the objects. She shakes her head and returns the objects. "Give me the third and fourth objects," she says. Again she tests for vibrations and returns these objects.

The process continues until she begins to zero in on the chosen object. She says, "Give me the fourth and eighth objects again." After a moment of thought, she says, "I've got it. You picked the pencil."

The trick can be repeated. The objects may be mixed around. The audience can substitute other objects for those on the table. Except for the words spoken by the medium, no one else speaks.

Method: One object codes the necessary information to the medium. It is the ruler. If, say, the spectator chooses the fourth object in the row, wait until your medium asks for the ruler and one other object. Grasp the ruler so that your thumbnail contacts the number 4, Figure 111. This tells the medium that the spectator chose the fourth object in the row.

Fig. 111

When she takes the ruler in her right hand and some other object in her left hand, she looks down the blindfold to see which number you are coding to her. She then goes on to pick different objects at random, until she decides she is ready to reveal the correct object. In this example, she would ask for the fourth object. When it is handed to her, she says, "This is the object you chose."

48. Think Alike Again

When you perform "Think Alike," there may be no ruler available, or the audience may decide to substitute some other object for the ruler. This method will produce exactly the same effect without the ruler. As before, nine or ten objects are placed in a row on the table. One is chosen. Your blindfolded medium asks for the objects two at a time. She then goes on to reveal the chosen object.

Method: When you hand the medium two objects, you touch her finger so that the finger you touch corresponds to the position of the chosen object in the row. If the chosen object is the first object in the row, you touch her right thumb. If it is the second object in the row, touch her right first finger. If it is the third object, touch her right middle finger, and so on.

49. Who Done It?

Whodunits are murder mysteries. This is an impromptu version in which your assistant, isolated in the next room, reveals the identity of the guilty party.

After your medium goes into an adjoining room, the door is closed so she is isolated from the scene of the crime. Hand a water pistol to a spectator. That person passes the pistol to someone else, and that person passes it to someone else. The process continues until one spectator decides that he is going to be the culprit.

You point to different people in random order. As you do, each person says his or her name so that your assistant can hear the name. Thus, she might hear "Brian," then "Mary," then "John," then "David," then "Jennifer," and so on until each person has been named.

Your assistant then announces, "Jennifer is the guilty party!" and she is right.

Someone can stand in front of the door to the room where your assistant is situated to prevent any suspicion that she is peeking through the keyhole. The trick may be repeated.

Method: Point first to a boy, then a girl, then a boy, then a girl. When you want to secretly signal the guilty party to your assistant, call out two boys in a row, or two girls in a row. The next person you point to is the guilty party. In the above example, you called out David, then Brian—two boys. Your assistant knows that the next person you point to (Jennifer in this example) is the guilty party.

If the trick is repeated, you may want to give it this twist. Explain that you will give each person an alias by switching around the names of those at the party, but that you will use the true name of the guilty party.

The system is the same as that described above. Call out a boy's name when you point to the first person, a girl's name when you point to the second person, a boy's name when you point to the next person, and so on. Thus, you might point to John and say, "Bob." Then you point to Carol and say, "Mary," Alternate the names as in the first version. When you want to signal that the guilty party is about to be named, say two boys' names or two girls' names in a row. Then call out the guilty party by his or her real name. Continue to call out more names. When you are finished, your assistant in the next room reveals the correct name of the culprit.

50. The Three-Object Test

You and your partner can perform a baffling mind-reading mystery using borrowed objects. This is a trick that may be repeated because the mystery deepens each time.

Three borrowed objects are gathered in a handkerchief or paper bag. The objects may be a watch, a cup and a pencil. Your medium sees the objects and handles them to receive psychic impressions.

The medium leaves the room. Someone removes one of the objects from the bag, shows it around and hides it behind his back.

The medium returns. She stares at the bag, walks around it, concentrates for a moment and correctly reveals the missing object.

For the second test, three different objects (say a spoon, a red handkerchief and a glove) are used. The medium correctly identifies the missing object.

The third test is the hardest because it uses similar objects—in this case, three borrowed coins: for example, a 1990 nickel, a 1988 penny and a 1993 dime. While the medium is out of the room, one of the coins is removed from the bag and hidden. She enters the room, concentrates for a moment and announces the date on the missing coin.

Method: If you had to secretly code the name of the object to the medium, you would have a difficult time because so many different objects could come into play. The method used here is much simpler. When the objects are placed in the bag one at a time, the medium need only remember that, for example, the

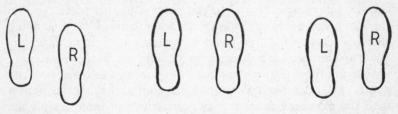

Fig. 112   Fig. 113   Fig. 114

watch went in first, the cup second, the pencil third. When an object is removed and hidden, you signal to the medium whether it is the first, second or third object. This is done as follows.

If it is the first object, stand with your left foot in front of your right foot, Figure 112. It if is the second object, stand so your feet are even, Figure 113. If it is the third object, stand so your right foot is in front of your left foot, Figure 114. In the case of the test with the three coins, have the date of each coin announced before it is dropped into the bag. The medium then remembers the order of the dates.

The medium may be blindfolded. When she is led back into the room, she looks down the blindfold at the position of your feet. The trick is more impressive if the medium takes her time revealing the hidden object. She can walk around the bag, stare in the direction of the bag, talk about the difficulty of receiving clear psychic impressions. When she announces the missing object, it is that much more dramatic. As with many mind-reading tricks, this is a good example of a simple secret being used to set up a big mystery.

51. Crime Does Not Pay

Like "Who Done It?" (No. 49), this is a murder mystery and one of the best. It is ideal for performance at a party at which there are a lot of guests. The medium is escorted to another room and the door closed. You pass around a stack of play-money one-million-dollar bills. Someone volunteers to play the part of a bank robber and hides the money in his pocket.

The medium enters the room, looks over the roomful of suspects and proceeds to walk directly to the guilty party and say, "You're under arrest."

Method: Once someone takes the money, stand off to the side. Act as if your part in the mystery is no longer important. What you do, however, is crucial to the success of this trick. Assume the same pose as the guilty party. In other words, if he is standing with his arms folded, you stand with your arms folded. If he sits down and crosses his right leg over his left, you do the same.

Your medium glances in your direction as she questions the guests. She sees the way you are situated and finds the person with the matching pose. It may be that two or more people are standing or sitting in exactly the same way as the guilty party.

Wait for the guilty party to shift his or her position. Change your position to match it. In the meantime, the medium can ask all sorts of questions, such as "What did you have for breakfast this morning?" or "Have you lost weight recently?" as if the answers could possibly lend a clue about the identity of the guilty party. She notices any change in the way you are standing or sitting and finds the person with the matching pose.

Money Magic

Coins and dollar bills are available anywhere. People are universally interested in money—earning it, investing it and spending it. Learn a few money tricks and you will always be able to entertain friends and family at a moment's notice.

52. Strongman Stuff

Rub a coin against your sleeve to increase and focus the magnetic field surrounding the coin (or so you claim). Then place the coin on top of your head.

Place your right hand against the coin as shown in Figure 115. While pressing your hand against the coin, invite the spectator to grasp your wrist.

Fig. 115

You claim that the magnetic field is so strong that the spectator will find it impossible to lift your hand from the coin. Try as he might, he cannot make your hand budge.

Method: Perform the trick exactly as written above. If you press down on the coin with firm, even pressure, the spectator will find it impossible to move your hand away from the coin.

74

53. By George, He Got It!

A spectator folds a quarter inside a dollar bill and gives it to you behind your back. You say, "Using mind power alone, I will tell you something about this coin that no one in this room could possibly know." You pause for a moment and then say, "The coin has George Washington's picture on it."

This is true, but not impressive; after all, Washington's picture is on most quarters. "By an odd coincidence, Washington's picture is also on the bill you gave me." This too is true but not surprising; Washington's picture is on *all* one-dollar bills.

"The part that no one knows is that the date on the coin is 1993. Even more interesting, the serial number on the bill is four, six, eight, three, nine, three, four, seven." The spectator examines the coin and the bill to discover that you are right.

Method: Beforehand, place a dollar bill on the table and jot down the serial number on your thumbnail. Memorize the date on the quarter. Fold the dollar bill around the quarter and tuck the package under your watchband. You will have to wear a long-sleeved shirt or jacket to make sure that the folded bill is concealed from audience view.

Ask a spectator to fold a quarter into a dollar bill. Turn your head aside as he does this, so it is clear that you do not see the numbers on the bill or the date on the coin.

Take the folded package and place it behind your back. Tell the spectator you will reveal something that no one could possibly know. Then say, "The coin has Washington's picture on it." He is not impressed, so you add, "Not only that; the dollar bill also has Washington's picture on it."

As you speak, silently remove the package from under your watch band and put the folded bill from the spectator in its place.

Say, "And not only *that*, the date on the coin is 1993," naming the date on your coin.

"Even more interesting, I can reveal the serial number on the dollar bill." Turn your back so the spectator can see the folded bill. Ask him to unfold the bill. With your back still toward the spectator, glance at the secret writing on your thumbnail and rattle off the serial number.

Instead of writing the serial number on your thumbnail, you can write it on a scrap of paper. Hide the paper near the telephone or on a bookshelf. When you perform the trick, let the spectator open the bill. Then pace back and forth, eventually working your way over to where the scrap of paper is hidden. Read off the serial number as you pretend to concentrate.

54. Guessing Game

This trick cannot be performed on all occasions, but in special circumstances it packs a big surprise.

You place a coin on your left palm and cover it with a handkerchief, Figure 116. Go to each of five or six different people in your audience. Each one places his hand under the handkerchief and tries to guess which coin is on your palm. The coin is a small one, so they will probably guess that it is either a penny or a dime.

When you remove the handkerchief, it is not a small coin the audience sees; the coin has mysteriously changed into a half-dollar, Figure 117.

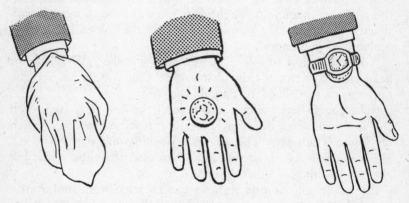

Fig. 116   Fig. 117   Fig. 118

Method: Beforehand, slide your wristwatch around so the watch face is against your wrist. Place a half-dollar under the watch, Figure 118. If the watch is large enough, the coin will be completely concealed. Otherwise you will have to wear a long-sleeved shirt or a jacket to conceal the coin.

You will also need a confederate, that is, someone who secretly helps you with this trick. He is the last person to put his hand under the handkerchief. We will get to him in a moment.

To present the trick, show the handkerchief on both sides.

Hold it in one hand. With the other hand, go into your pocket and get a dime. Do not show the coin. Say you want to try a guessing game. Hold the coin in your clenched fist. Cover your hand with the handkerchief.

When your hand has been covered, open your fingers. Let each of five or six people reach under the handkerchief and try to guess what the coin is. The last person is your confederate. When he puts his hand under the handkerchief, he slides the half-dollar out from under the wristwatch and covers the dime with it.

Say, "Gee, I didn't think it was that hard to figure out what the coin was." Remove the handkerchief, revealing that the small coin everyone thought it was is actually a half-dollar.

You do not want anyone to know that you have a dime concealed under the half-dollar. At the end of the trick, close your hand into a fist and place the coins into your pocket as you take your bow. There is one other point to remember. Make sure the handkerchief or scarf is large enough and thick enough to provide ample cover for the confederate's secret work.

55. Watch George

The magician shows a dollar bill with George Washington's picture right side up, Figure 119. He slowly folds the bill into eighths. When he unfolds it, the bill is upside down, Figure 120.

Method: Hold a dollar bill with the picture of George Washington facing the audience as in Figure 121, shown in the magician's

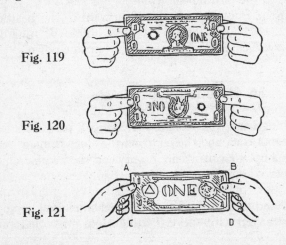

Fig. 119

Fig. 120

Fig. 121

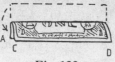

Fig. 122

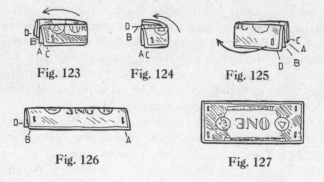

Fig. 123   Fig. 124   Fig. 125

Fig. 126   Fig. 127

view. Fold the top half over in front, Figure 122. Then fold the right side over onto the left side, Figure 123. Finally, fold the right half over onto the left. The bill has now been folded into eighths, Figure 124.

Now you are going to unfold the bill. It will look to the audience like a reversal of the folding procedure, but there is an important difference.

Unfold the portion of the bill nearest you in the direction of the arrow in Figure 124 to begin the unfolding process. The result is shown in Figure 125. Now unfold the portion of the bill nearest you in the direction of the arrow shown in Figure 125. You will then be at the position shown in Figure 126.

Finally, bring the front half of the bill upward to the position shown in Figure 127. The bill is completely unfolded, but from the audience view, George Washington is now upside down.

56. Bare-handed Vanish

In this astonishing trick, you roll up your sleeves, pass a scarf or handkerchief over a coin, and the coin vanishes into thin air. Your sleeves are rolled up, your hands are empty and the handkerchief may be borrowed. Where did the coin go?

Method: You should be wearing a long-sleeved shirt. Roll up your sleeves. Display a coin with the left hand. Hold a handkerchief with the right hand. The starting position is shown in Figure 128.

Bring the handkerchief in front of the coin so that the coin is hidden from the audience's view. Unknown to them, the coin is slipped under the right thumb as shown in Figure 129.

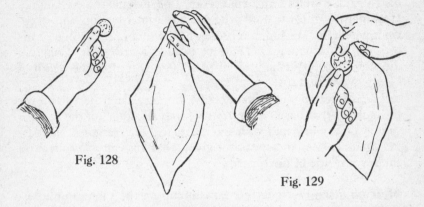

Fig. 128

Fig. 129

Do not hesitate as you make this move. The secret transfer of the coin should be practiced until it can be done smoothly and without fumbling. The right hand then moves up the left arm, so that the handkerchief slides over the left hand. When the handkerchief is just above the sleeve, the right hand releases the coin so that it drops into the rolled-up portion of the left sleeve, Figure 130. Do not stop here; keep moving the right hand back toward the body until the handkerchief is clear of the left hand. The left hand has remained stationary all along. As the handkerchief clears the left hand, the audience realizes that the coin has vanished. Show both hands front and back. Drop the handkerchief to the table. Take your bow.

Fig. 130

57. Spirit of '76

George Washington's ghost makes an unexpected appearance in this trick. Four quarters are shown front and back. One is placed on the table before the spectator. The magician asks George Washington's ghost to guide the spectator in answering this question; which did Washington prefer, his home in Mt. Vernon or his office in Washington, D.C.? (This is itself a little joke. Congress did not meet in Washington until 1800, a year after the death of George Washington.)

The spectator might choose Mt. Vernon. When he turns over the quarter that has been in front of him all along, on the reverse side is a piece of paper with the message, "Mt. Vernon." No matter which answer the spectator gives, that answer will appear on the reverse side of the quarter.

Method: Place four quarters tail-side up on the table. Put adhesive stickers on the two center quarters. If adhesive stickers are not available, you can glue circular disks of plain white paper to the quarters. On one disk write, "Mt. Vernon," and on the other, "Washington D.C." as shown in Figure 131.

Fig. 131

Stack the quarters on top of one another so the quarters with the message are in the center. This preparation is done secretly. When you are ready to present the trick, grasp the stack of quarters between the left thumb and first finger as shown in Figure 132. The quarters are tail-side up and the hand is palm up.

Show the stack as you say, "This is a quiz involving George Washington's favorite hangout. We will use these beautiful images of Washington."

Turn the hand palm down, Figure 133, bringing the stack head-side up. Take the top quarter from the stack, Figure 134, and place it head-side up on the table.

Turn the left hand back to the position shown in Figure 132, bringing the tail side of the stack uppermost. Display the stack, then turn the hand palm down, Figure 133. Remove the next quarter and place it heads up on the table.

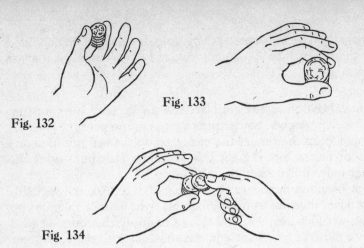

Fig. 132

Fig. 133

Fig. 134

Repeat the same sequence for each of the other two quarters. There is an odd illusion at work here. It will look to the audience as if you showed the front and back of *each* quarter as the hand swings back and forth between the positions shown in Figures 132 and 133.

Ask George Washington's ghost to help the spectator answer this question correctly: Did George Washington prefer to be at home in Mt. Vernon or at work in Washington, D.C.? Whatever the spectator's answer, grasp the quarter that has the same answer written on the back and slide it toward the spectator. Put the other three quarters in your pocket.

Ask him to turn over the quarter. He will be surprised to see a message, and even more surprised that it matches his answer.

As an aid in remembering which quarter has which message, use quarters with different dates. You can keep three extra quarters in the pocket. If the spectator asks to see the quarters, or if you wish to use these coins for your next trick, bring out the three unprepared quarters.

58. Pocket Presto

In this remarkable trick, you ask a friend to empty the change from his pocket while you turn your back. He chooses any coin except a penny and places it in his right pocket. Then he places the rest of the change into his left pocket.

After he performs a few quick calculations, you tell him how much change he has in each pocket! This is a good example of a trick that can be performed at any time. It can even be done over the telephone, since you do not have to be present in the room to perform it.

Method: Have the spectator place any single coin except a penny into his right pocket. Say he puts a dime in the pocket. Then ask him to add up the rest of the change and jot down the total on a piece of paper. Say the total is 37 cents. He then hides this change in his left pocket.

Your back has been turned to the audience. Ask the spectator to jot down the value of the coin in his right pocket. In our example he would write "10." Have him multiply this number by 2, getting 20. When he has done this, he adds 5 to the result, getting 25. Then he multiplies this new number by 50 (25 × 50 =1250, in our example).

Ask him to add to this total the amount of change he has in his left pocket (1250 + 37 = 1287). Then ask him to announce the grand total to you.

You arrive at the amount of change in each pocket by this secret process. Subtract 250 from his total. In our example it would look like this: 1287 − 250 = 1037. You know that the coin in his right pocket can have one of the values 5, 10 or 25; that is, it must be either a nickel, a dime or a quarter. The two leftmost digits of 1037 are 10. This tells you that the spectator has a 10-cent piece, or a dime, in his right pocket.

The remaining digits are 37. This tells you that the spectator has 37 cents in his left pocket.

To take another example, if the spectator has chosen to place a nickel in his right pocket and 42 cents in his left pocket, he would perform the calculations and announce that his total is 792. Secretly subtract 250 to arrive at 542. The "5" on the left tells you he has a 5-cent piece, or a nickel, in his right pocket. The 42 on the right tells you he has 42 cents in his left pocket.

It is not always easy to perform mental calculations when doing tricks before an audience. "Pocket Presto" may be performed with the spectator in one room and you in another. Explain that if you are isolated from him, you can have no clue as to the amount of change in his pockets. When he announces the grand total to you, you can perform the necessary calculation with pen and paper, or with a pocket calculator. Then enter the room where the spectator is and announce how much change he has in each pocket.

The trick can also be done over the telephone. Call someone you want to impress with your magical abilities. Have them perform the calculations described above and announce the result to you over the phone. You have a calculator handy and have already entered − 250 into it. Enter the spectator's number with a plus sign and immediately you know how much change he has in each pocket.

59. Cloak of Invisibility

Many of the tricks in this book produce a single effect. "Cloak of Invisibility" routines together two tricks; a coin is first made to vanish into thin air, then it magically becomes visible again.

Holding up a handkerchief or scarf, you say, "This is a cloak of invisibility. It seems to work best with coins." Borrow a quarter. Ask the spectator to note the date on the coin so he will recognize it when it is returned to him.

Hold the quarter in one hand, a glass in the other, Figure 135. The audience sees you drop the quarter into the glass and cover it with the handkerchief.

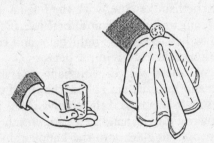

Fig. 135

"It takes six seconds to work." Wait six seconds, then withdraw the glass from under the handkerchief. Toss the coin into the air. It seems to vanish in plain sight of the audience.

The invisible coin is caught and dumped back into the glass. With a loud "Clink!" it becomes visible again.

Method: Place a drinking glass mouth down on the table. Drape a handkerchief or scarf over the left hand. Grasp a borrowed quarter or other coin through the handkerchief. Grip the bottom of the glass with the right hand palm down and turn the hand palm up. The situation is shown in Figure 135.

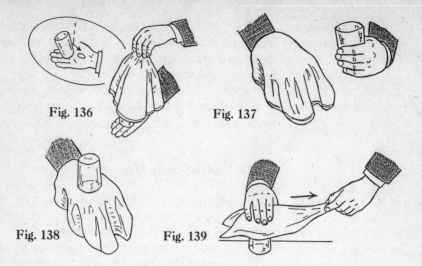

Fig. 136

Fig. 137

Fig. 138

Fig. 139

Turn the left hand palm down as you bring the coin to a position over the glass, Figure 136. Pretend to drop the coin into the glass. You actually tilt the glass on an angle so the coin hits the side of the glass and falls onto the palm. This is shown by the arrow in Figure 136.

Reach under the handkerchief with the left hand. Gently slide the glass out from under the handkerchief, Figure 137. The handkerchief now lies flat on the right palm and covers the coin. The audience thinks the coin is in the glass.

Make a tossing motion with the left hand, as if tossing the coin out of the glass and into the air. Follow the flight of the invisible coin with the eyes. It seems as if the coin vanishes in midflight.

Extend the palm-up right hand as if catching the invisible coin on the palm. Invert the glass onto the handkerchief, Figure 138. Say, "That's how we trap an invisible coin."

Grip the glass through the handkerchief with the right hand. Turn the apparatus over and place it on the table. The right hand remains on top of the glass to hide the coin from audience view.

Gently pull the handkerchief out of the way with the left hand, Figure 139, as you say, "To make the coin visible again, we have to take the cloak of invisibility away." When the handkerchief is taken away, the coin will fall into the glass. Do not forget to give the coin back to its owner.

Once the handling becomes familiar to you, you may wish to substitute a ring or other small object for the coin. A mysterious talisman or good-luck charm will suggest other patter possibilities.

Confederates

A confederate is someone who aids the magician without the audience's knowledge. He pretends to be an innocent onlooker, but he plays a vital role in the performance. Use confederates sparingly. They will help you produce some strong magical mysteries, but if used too frequently, they will attract suspicion. Reserve the use of a confederate for just the right occasion to enhance your reputation as a performer of real magic.

60. Numbers in Mind

You will need the help of three people for this test in mind reading. One spectator chooses a three-digit number and does a little figuring. The second spectator covers the writing with a cup. The third spectator places his hand on top of the cup to make sure it is not moved or tampered with.

You have been out of the room during this time. When you return, you stare at the ceiling as if studying the thought waves floating around. Then you slowly reveal the hidden numbers. The trick may be repeated one more time.

Method: One of the three spectators is a confederate. We will describe his part in this mystery in a moment. First we will describe the way the number is chosen.

While you turn your back or are out of the room, the first spectator silently decides on a three-digit number. Each digit should be different from the others, and from 1 to 9 (in other words, he does not choose zero). Ask him to jot down the number on a pad. Then ask him to reverse the number. Finally, have him subtract the smaller number from the larger.

For example, he might choose the number 835. He reverses this to get 538. Then he subtracts the smaller number from the larger: 835 − 538 = 297. The number you will reveal is 297. It is done as follows.

The second spectator is your confederate. He codes to you a small but vital piece of information. The confederate picks up the cup and uses it to cover the numbers. But he does this in a special way. Picture the paper as if it were a clock dial with the numbers 1 through 12 around the border. The confederate is going to secretly let you know the first digit in the spectator's answer. He does this by pointing the handle of the cup at the same number on the invisible clock. In our example, the first digit in the spectator's answer is 2. The handle of the cup is therefore placed as shown in Figure 140. (The numbers are shown in Figure 140 only to illustrate the imaginary clock dial. In practice there are no numbers. Thus, if the confederate wanted to indicate the number 3, he would point the handle of the cup as shown in Figure 141.)

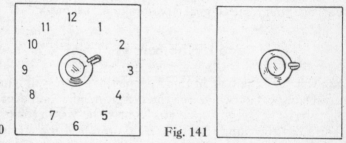

Fig. 140   Fig. 141

The third spectator's task is to place his hand on top of the cup to make sure no one can peek under the cup at the numbers.

When you return to the room, spot the position of the cup handle. From this you know the first digit in the answer. The second digit is always 9, and the third digit is the difference between the first digit and 9. If the first digit is 2, for example, the third digit is 7. The three digits are thus 2, 9, 7. Knowing all three digits, you are then in a position to reveal the numbers in a dramatic manner.

On rare occasions the first digit will be 0. This will occur if the spectator chose the number 423, for example: 423 − 324 = 099. Your confederate signals the situation by pointing the cup handle straight up at what would be the 12 o'clock position on the imaginary clock dial.

61. Guilty Party

Like "Who Done It?" (No. 49) and "Crime Does Not Pay" (No. 51), this is a murder mystery. When you go out of the room, a toy gun is passed around until someone decides they want to be the guilty party. He hides the gun in his pocket. Then someone else jots down on a pad a list of possible suspects, including the guilty party.

You enter the room and pass the list around. "Do you see your name on this list?" you ask. The spectator says yes. "Do you have an alibi for the time this crime was committed?" The spectator replies yes again.

You ask each suspect the same questions. Then you take back the pad, study it a moment, and reveal the name of the guilty party.

No verbal code is used. You do not know the names on the list until the pad is handed to you. The names can be written in any order. You can repeat the trick immediately with a new list of suspects. You will always find the guilty party.

Method: Your confederate is one of the people to whom you hand the list of suspects. She scans the list and sees that, for example, the guilty party is the fourth name on the list. She then puts four fingers on the back of the pad, Figure 142. You have been standing with your back to her, pretending to study the faces of other suspects. When you take back the pad, spot the number of fingers she has used to signal you. After you have spoken to all the suspects, look at the fourth name on the list and announce that he or she is the culprit.

If, for example, the culprit's name is sixth on the list, your confederate would use two hands, Figure 143, to signal you.

Fig. 142   Fig. 143

62. A Mind for Money

Place a penny, nickel, dime and quarter on the table. While you turn your back, a spectator chooses a coin by silently turning it over. With your back still turned, ask someone to hand you a piece of paper and a pen behind your back. You make a few squiggly lines on the paper to get your thoughts in focus. Then you write "nickel" on the paper. Ask the spectator which coin he chose. He will admit that he chose the nickel.

Method: The spectator who hands you the pen and paper is a confederate. If he hands you the pen with the cap on it, it means the penny was chosen. If he takes the cap off and puts it on the opposite end of the pen before handing it to you, the nickel was chosen. If he takes the cap off and hands you the pen without the cap, the dime was chosen. Finally, if he says he does not have a pen, it means the quarter was chosen. In this case you can borrow a pen from someone else, or do without and simply reveal the chosen coin.

If you do the same trick on another occasion for the same audience, it is wise to have a substitute method at hand. One way is for the confederate to have a pencil stub in one pocket, a longer pencil in another, a still longer pencil in another and a full-size pencil in another pocket. You and he agree beforehand that the pencil stub indicates the penny, the next larger pencil the nickel, and so on.

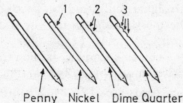

Fig. 144   Penny   Nickel   Dime Quarter

Still another method uses four pencils of equal length. The smooth pencil in Figure 144 codes a penny; the pencil with a notch near the top codes a nickel; the pencil with two notches codes a dime; the pencil with three notches codes a quarter.

It is sometimes wise to teach one method to one confederate, and a different method to another confederate. If both confederates happen to be present at your performance, one of them will be in the know, but the other will be fooled by a secret he does not know.

63. The Nine-Cent Card Trick

This is a card trick that uses nine pennies. Ask a spectator to shuffle nine cards and deal them out as shown in Figure 145. While you turn your back, he chooses a card and places a penny on it. Ask him to remember the date on the coin.

Fig. 145

Another spectator shakes up eight more pennies and places one on each of the remaining cards. You turn around and study the coins. Then you announce, "You picked a penny with the date 1993." If the spectator asks you to reveal the card he picked, you can do that too.

This is a trick done under strong performing conditions. The cards are shuffled and dealt in any order. The spectator can pick any card and any coin. Nevertheless, when you turn around, you reveal the chosen coin, the chosen card or both.

Method: One of the cards must be a ten-spot. It does not matter what the other eight cards are. The coins can be any nine pennies. The spectator who shakes up the coins and places one on each card is a confederate.

The code makes use of the spots on the ten-spot. Think of the spots on this card as being numbered according to the system shown in Figure 146. Each number stands for one of the cards in the layout. If the spectator picked the first card in the layout (the ♦ 2 in Figure 145), your confederate would place a penny on the first pip of the ten-spot, Figure 147. If he chose the second card (the ♥6 in our example), your confederate would place the penny on the second pip, Figure 148.

| Fig. 146 | Fig. 147 | Fig. 148 |

When you turn around, pretend to study all of the cards and coins, but actually glance at the position of the coin that rests on the ten-spot. From this you know the chos-en card. The coin resting on the chosen card is the chosen coin. Remember the date on this coin.

Reveal the date on this coin. If the coin is tails up, turn over several of the coins, including the chosen coin. Then note the date. Look away from the layout and say, "I'm getting a picture of the date on the penny you chose. I see a one and a nine. Am I right so far?" Of course you are since all coins in circulation have a 1 and a 9 as the first two numbers. "The rest is harder. Wait, it's clear now, another nine and a three. Was the date nineteen ninety-three?"